WALKING
WITH
Tension

Jennifer Christine Hill

Foreword by
Steve Wiens

To Jesus,
the author of my faith,
and the true author of this story.
Thanks for walking with me.

❧ Author's Note ❧

This story was written from my best recollection of memories.
It is true. However, some details have been changed or combined
to protect the identity of characters in the story, or to help
the flow of the story itself. When actual names were used,
they were used with permission.

Foreword

If you are a Christian who is experiencing the disappointment and disillusionment that comes with unexplained pain and suffering, you have most likely received two kinds of responses from fellow Christians. Neither one of them helps, and yet you hear them with such frequency that you wonder if everybody's reading the same faulty instruction manual entitled "How to Simultaneously Dismiss and Offend Those Who Suffer," which nobody has had the decency to burn, or at least rewrite.

Response number one involves people who seem to be more concerned with defending the character of God than walking alongside you in your pain. Their opening arguments begin with the insistence that God is all-powerful, all-knowing, and all-good. God both initiates and allows your suffering because a greater plan is in the works. They will carefully remind you that even though you can't see it, and don't know it, God must have a reason for your pain. God, after all, is in control, and your job is not to understand but to simply shrug your shoulders and wait until God's plan finally unfolds.

Response number two involves pressure to follow an immediate action plan through which your suffering will stop. This involves following a formula which, if followed exactly, will relieve you of your pain as soon as you simply put it to action. You hear stories of people who were "just like you" and now are completely healed. Your hopes are raised and then dashed when these formulas fail. You feel betrayed by God, horribly defective because nothing "works" on you, and perhaps your friends have even given up on you because you must not have enough faith.

In *Walking with Tension*, Jenny Hill follows neither path. Instead, she blazes a new trail entirely. She tells her courageous story of learning to live with cerebral palsy, wrestling and engaging with God all along the way. Her story is captivating because it is raw and in some ways, disappointing. I cried my way through this manuscript, at times yelling at characters in her life that responded to her in ways that were damaging and unhelpful. Jenny writes poignantly and honestly about her struggle to make friends in junior high school while maintaining her identity through excelling in academics. She tells of her relationship with a Christian "healer" who promised results that never came. She writes passionately about both her belief and her unbelief. She teaches us that becoming fully alive in God is a course in which we all must enroll, whatever challenges our life may present.

In the end, *Walking with Tension* is a story of beauty and redemption. Jenny is learning how to honestly grapple with the disappointing reality that some things are not healed, but she's also learning to gratefully and eagerly accept the gifts that God has given her in her unique journey. God's gentle friendship, healing, and consistent leading has marked Jenny in deep and profound ways, and her journey blazes a new trail for those of us who are struggling to find God in our suffering.

If you are a Christian who is experiencing pain and suffering, this book is not the answer for you. But it is the story of a very courageous person who is learning that God accompanies her in her pain, that God is partnering with her in discovering how her redemption is helping other people to grow and heal, and that healing is sometimes found as one learns to walk out one's pain and suffering not with resolution, but with tension.

– Steve Wiens, Associate Senior Pastor, Church of the Open Door

Chapter 1

It was just after 8:30 PM when I heard the familiar sound of the garage door lifting from where I lay on the other side of the wall. Mom and Dad had gone to hear a speaker for the evening and weren't expected back until later. The muffled sound of the TV came up from the basement where my older brother Gabe was watching. I heard the front door slowly opening below me and then my dad's voice, calling to Gabe, "Where's Jenny?"

"She's upstairs sleeping."

"She's in bed already?" I heard the surprise in my dad's voice, followed by the sound of his footsteps as he climbed the stairs towards my room. 8:30 was early for me to go to bed, but on that particular evening, I was feverish and chilly, wanting to rest so I could feel better. I hadn't been able to fall asleep, so I lay in bed, tossing and turning. Staring now at my bedroom door, anticipating my dad's entry, I watched as the handle turned.

"Hi Dad," I mumbled from my bed. I had turned over on my stomach, letting one arm dangle to the floor. My fingers were tracing the threads in the carpet. Not only was I sick, I was bored. At the sight of my dad, I propped myself up on my elbows and gave him my full attention. "What are you doing back so soon?"

My dad knelt down beside my bed. He looked down at the floor for a minute, paused, and then looked into my eyes. I searched his face, trying to understand the reason for his hesitation. There was a look in his eyes that I couldn't recognize. Was it sadness? After a brief pause, my dad began to speak. "Jenny, the speaker your mom and I went to hear tonight prays for people to get healed."

Like Jesus did in the Bible? I wondered as I laid there, surprised and confused. I leaned a little closer into the words my dad was saying, wondering what he was going to say next.

"I came home early tonight because I was wondering if you wanted me to take you to see him." My dad again returned his gaze to the floor while I considered what I had just heard. I felt like Samuel, being pulled from bed after hearing the voice of God. *Do miracles still happen today?* My mind began to recall stories from Sunday school of Jesus reaching out to heal people who were crippled, telling them to "Take up their mats and walk!" I never thought of myself as someone who was crippled like the people in those stories or even as someone who was in need of healing or a miracle, but I did have cerebral palsy—a condition that had no cure. *Why not go? What can it hurt? If this is what God wants, I wouldn't mind not having CP for the rest of my life. If it doesn't work, what's there to lose?*

Willing to take the risk and a little skeptical of the outcome, I answered my dad with a nod, "Sure I'll go. Just give me a minute."

"Take all the time you need," he said as he left the room for me to change.

I got out of bed and walked over to my dresser. I was wearing my brother's old bathrobe and sporting a T-shirt underneath that my mom had bought at a garage sale. It was white with red lettering that read *Betty's Dance Studio*. I'd never taken dance lessons, in fact my body was rather uncoordinated, but I loved the idea of dancing so I had asked her to buy it for me. I pulled on some denim shorts that were once full-length jeans and placed some brown sunglasses on my head to act as a headband. After pulling on some sandals, I was ready to go.

As I was about to leave my room, I stopped and stood in the threshold of my doorway, running my hand up over the frame, pausing before heading downstairs to meet my dad. I thought about when I was four, immobilized in a full body cast after extensive surgery to correct my gait. I had a hard time falling asleep while I was in my cast, so I used to sing songs to God that I had learned in Sunday school. I was comforted even though I didn't fully understand who God was at such a young age. My mind raced forward to first grade where I remembered the pain of loneliness that I carried within the depths of my soul because I didn't have any friends. I remembered walking down the hallway one day at school, praying for friends, for someone to like me, when I heard what I thought was the voice of God, almost whispering gently in my ear: "I will be your friend." It was at that moment that I began to realize that even though I felt lonely, I was never alone. God loved me and was walking beside me.

Sometime later, I stood at the very doorway where I was standing now as I asked God to come into my room, into my heart, into my very life, and be with me. God was knocking at my heart, so I stood in the doorway of my room, responding the only way I knew how, in order to answer His call and welcome Him. Just like I knew I was precious to my dad, I also knew that I was precious to God; I was His special little girl, the apple of His eye. Not only did He love me, I was convinced He liked me because He seemed to show up when I needed Him most. Maybe tonight was one of those special times, where God was offering His gentle friendship, extending His hand to deliver me from my awkwardness, saving me from the pain of having to live the rest of my life with cerebral palsy.

I drew my hand away from the door frame and headed down to meet my dad who was waiting for me in the car. We sat there in silence for a few moments, neither one of us quite sure what to say to the other. As we neared the first intersection, my dad tried to prepare me for the experience. He asked me what *I* was going to say to this speaker. *Me? Wasn't this his idea? I am only twelve—shouldn't he be the one talking?*

"What do you mean?" I asked.

He told me the story of blind Bartimaeus in reply. "Before Jesus healed Bartimaeus, he asked him one question: 'What do you want me to do for you?' Bartimaeus, relieved to be heard above the crowd, said for all to hear that he wanted to see again. Then Jesus healed him." Dad turned to me. "The man you are going to meet will ask what you want from God. What're you going to say?"

I was silent, letting the reality of the story—and his questions—sink in. They scared me. Where some people saw Jesus' question as simple, to me, a little girl with CP longing for a normal life, it was terrifying. It was as if Jesus approached Bartimaeus with a sneer, saying, "You want to be physically healed? Fine, but first you have to publicly humiliate yourself by telling everyone here what you struggle with even though it's obvious." When I heard that story, I only felt shame. Shame for Bartimaeus. And shame for myself. To say out loud why I wasn't like other people—and to ask for that to go away in front of a crowd of healthy people—frightened me. It was extremely vulnerable and shaming. I was already very self-conscious about CP and the barriers it put up between me and others. Talking about it in public—whether to a stranger or friend—was hard and awkward. I never knew what to say or how to act. But if that's what it took for me to be healed, to be normal, then I would do it.

Taking a deep breath, I looked right at my dad. I knew what he wanted me to say. "I'm going to tell him that I want to be healed of cerebral palsy." My words were confident, but inside I was growing uneasy. The hope that bubbled up in me moments before was bursting under this new twist.

Too soon we arrived at a high school auditorium full of people. My dad took my hand and walked me down a side aisle leading up to the stage. As we walked forward, I could feel several eyes in the audience staring at me, as if they were awaiting my arrival. I kept my eyes on the ground, watching my steps as I walked. When we got to the steps leading up to the stage, I gripped my dad's hand, leaning on it for support. Once on stage, I looked to my left to see the man my dad had told me about. He was tall with blonde hair and a beard. He was wearing a suit and a headset microphone, which he spoke into with a very distinct British accent. He was finishing up praying for a couple who were standing on stage while I waited on the side. As soon as he was done, he looked up and made eye contact with my dad.

"Is this your daughter?" he gestured towards me.

"Yes, this is Jenny," my dad answered, placing his hand on my shoulder, leading me closer to the man. As we walked forward, I felt anxious anticipation building up in my stomach. I was getting closer to the moment when I would have to say the words "cerebral palsy" out loud, to this man, in front of hundreds of people. I didn't want to say the words, and yet some part of me was eager to publicly announce that I had a disability if this man could actually do something to change my condition.

"Hi Jenny," the British man was now looking down on me, smiling into my eyes. "My name is Ian."

"Hi," I said, waiting uncomfortably for him to ask the question Dad had told me about in the car. I crossed my legs while standing, bracing myself with more support.

"I had cancer when I was a kid," Ian explained, "but God healed me. I've been cancer free for over 20 years." Ian paused, "What would you like God to do for you?"

Letting go of all inhibition, blocking out all the eyes that were glued on me listening to our conversation, I let my request burst forth from my mouth, expressing my desire from the depths of my heart. "I want to be healed of cerebral palsy," I confessed in a rush. I paused, taking in the silence and the reality of what I had just said. To my amazement, naming my disability aloud didn't hurt as much as I thought it would. I felt relief, knowing that the moment was now over.

"Ok," Ian said with a nod and a smile. "Come over here." Ian took my hand and led me a few feet away from my dad to an empty spot near the center of the stage. I looked out towards the audience, trying to see who was in front of me, but the lights from the stage blinded my vision after the first few rows. Everyone was watching. It was as if the whole meeting had stopped in honor of this moment. I began to relax, realizing that the people in the audience were with me. They too had heard my request and were waiting with anticipation to see what God was going to do.

"Can I place my hand on your shoulder?" Ian asked.

"Yes," I reply, bowing my head in silence, listening intently as God heard Ian's prayer.

"Father, in the name of Jesus, I ask you to touch Jenny. Heal her body of cerebral palsy." *Whoosh!* Ian blew into his microphone, as if the sound he was making would help his request transfer to my body. I opened my eyes as his voice grew dim, but stood there silently, waiting. Nothing had happened. I certainly didn't feel any different, so I wondered what I was supposed to do next. Maybe healing took some time to set in or maybe there was another prayer that Ian had planned to pray. I wasn't sure, neither was the audience. I looked up at him for more direction.

"I want you to lay down right here," Ian instructed. This seemed to me like a strange request, but I did as I was told. A woman came over and draped a cloth over my body like a blanket and folded another one up to place under my head. It was good to be lying down again. My face felt hot from the heat of the lights and the rising temperature of my body. I felt dizzy once again as my body shifted its equilibrium as it changed from standing up to lying down. *Oh yeah, I'm sick,* I remembered. The events of the past few moments had temporarily taken my mind off my flu, but now that Ian's prayer was over, I once again became aware of the chills that ran up and down my arms and legs.

Ian knelt down by my side so we could see each other face to face. "How are you feeling?" *Awkward and out of place,* part of me wanted to answer. *Could I really be lying on a stage right now after asking God to heal me from something that had no cure?* The whole evening was beginning to feel surreal. I looked to my left.

My mom was sitting a few feet beside me, having silently joined us up on stage. Tears filled her eyes and dropped to the floor of the stage. *Why was my mom crying?* I couldn't understand her emotion—it just added to the growing bizarreness of the evening.

I'm really tired and I just want to go home. It seemed clear to me that God wasn't choosing heal me this evening, not only of my cerebral palsy but also of my flu. I discovered that the strongest thing I was experiencing at that moment was exhaustion. As I lay on the floor of the stage, wrapped in a blanket, I began to realize that my forehead was hot and sweaty. I was fighting fatigue as the hour grew late and was too overwhelmed by feelings of sickness to be disappointed at what had happened that night. More than anything, I longed to return to my bedroom, to wipe this evening from my memory like a faded dream. And yet, as I laid on the stage, trying to decide how to answer Ian, knowing that many eyes were looking at me, waiting for me to speak, I became increasingly aware of something subtle, yet very real and calming. I felt as though I was being wrapped in an embrace as secure as the blanket that covered my body. In the midst of the dramatic events that had taken place during this peculiar evening, it seemed that a quiet encore was taking place on stage. God was once again showing up in my life, making Himself and His love known to me through the gift of His quiet presence. It settled my body and drew my mind away from all the lights, attention, and anticipation that surrounded me. I could have fallen asleep on that stage, cocooned from to the world, because the presence of God felt so….

"Good." I finally replied.

"Good," Ian said, repeating my answer. He then turned to the audience and closed the meeting. I lay behind him, content, still in awe and wonder of this calming hug I seemed to be receiving from God. It was getting late, but as I laid there on the wooden stage beneath the lights, I began to wonder if perhaps tonight was not an end to a brief story with a disappointing climax, but rather the beginning of a journey to discover how God was going to heal me, someday, of cerebral palsy. I looked at my watch and found that it was already after 10:00 PM. The details of the evening were growing hazy in my mind. I slowly sat up and uncovered my body. Glancing around the stage, I quickly found my parents. Without saying a word, we all looked at each other and knew it was time to go home. As soon as we got to the car, I climbed into the backseat and shut my eyes. My mind was filled with wonder, but I was soon overcome with sleep. The questions I held for God would have to wait until another day.

Chapter 2

*A*s the week faded into the weekend, my flu began to subside. I was able to join my family in church on Sunday. We attended a small evangelical church made up mostly of growing families. The service was the same every week: announcements, prayer, music, and a sermon. Sitting in the pew on Sunday morning, listening to the pastor preach, was usually a boring activity, a time where I found myself doodling all over the pages of the bulletin that was handed out each week with my markers or a pen that I borrowed from my mom. While scribbling, I kept one ear open to my pastor's sermons. Week after week, I listened as he spoke on topics found in the Bible, such as prayer, the End Times, and preaching the gospel to the whole world. Occasionally, he would throw in an obscure passage from the Old Testament about people who had crazy names, and once, he even talked about sex! He had to warn everyone a week ahead of time in case families didn't want their children to hear, but on the following Sunday, the sanctuary had never been more full of teenagers!

Today, while I found the sermon to be routine, my interest was piqued. It was as if I had discovered a new color in the rainbow because of the events during the last week, except as I sat in the pew listening, doodling, I realized that this color was strikingly absent from the spectrum that lay before me. Worse yet, no one seemed to notice! Questions began to rise up in me at an alarming rate: *Why hadn't I ever heard my pastor talk about healing and miracles in one of his sermons?* I began to wonder what he would say about them if given the chance. *Why didn't we pray for people who were sick at the end our services?* Sure, there were requests for prayers listed each week in the bulletin from people who had cancer or were currently in the hospital. From time to time, we even prayed for these people aloud as a congregation, but I had never seen my pastor, or anyone else, touch someone gently on the shoulder and publicly ask God for healing. *Why not? Doesn't God work like that?* However, the biggest questions I held in my heart as I sat on the pew that Sunday morning, the ones that made it ache with hope and heavy with longing were these: *Was there anyone in my church who could understand what just happened to me this week? Was there anyone who could explain if God still performed* miracles? Would anyone help me find out whether God planned to heal me of cerebral palsy? Though I really wanted to know the answers to these questions, I was afraid to discover them alone.

As I sat in my pew at church, quietly pondering, I looked down at the bulletin that I held in my hands. I had doodled on much of it, taking a few notes as the morning went along. I flipped it over to check out the topic for youth group on Wednesday night. *Mark 10:51: Lessons from Bartimaeus.* My heart began to feel just a little bit lighter. I couldn't believe my eyes! My new youth pastor, John Peterson, was going to talk about the very man my dad had mentioned in the car! I didn't know him well, but perhaps he would be the one to help me on my journey.

"Listen to what happened to Jesus and Bartimaeus in Mark 10:51." It was Wednesday night, and I was huddled in a circle with other students during youth group. Our church was small, so we rented out the local middle school during the week to hold our meetings. Consequently, I found myself in a home economics room sitting on a blue, hard plastic school chair listening to John Peterson explain the New Testament story. I sat on the edge of my seat, eagerly waiting to hear his insight. I had spent the past two days studying the passage at home, wanting to learn all I could about this man whose experience, I felt, was similar to mine. John began to read from our handout: "Jesus asked him, 'What do you want me to do for you?' That's a basic question, right?" John asked us. *No, it's not a basic question!* I looked up from my paper and into John's eyes, following him as he paced the room speaking, wanting to interrupt and plead my point of view, but I sat there silently instead, fidgeting in my chair, waiting to give my rebuttal. Why in the world would Jesus ask him that? I passionately wondered. Why did He shame Bartimaeus by making him name his condition aloud? Everyone knew what was wrong!

"Why did Jesus ask him this?" John continued, "He asked so that Bartimaeus had the chance to announce his faith publicly." My pastor's perspective caused me to stop and think. *Was public confession really a necessary part of our faith? Did John understand how desperate it is tell everyone about your limitations in front of a crowd of people?* He was presenting this story as if Jesus was somehow doing Bartimaeus a favor by letting him speak, but it seemed to me that Bartimaeus was put on the spot, that he had no choice. Confusion continued to rise in me, but I kept my lips silent while I let my pastor conclude. "Here's the amazing thing," John paused, getting the room's full attention, "Jesus asks everyone this same question every day. He's asking you right now, 'What do you want me to do for you?' And what's your answer? What do you want Jesus to do in your life right now?"

The room suddenly became silent. I knew what the answer to that question was for me—I wanted to be healed of cerebral palsy, just like Bartimaeus was healed of his blindness. What I wasn't sure of was if God still approached people today and performed miracles like He did in the Bible. Was there even a chance that God wanted to heal me, and if there was, what did I need to do? Make a public confession? I had already done that. Pray harder? I looked down at the paper that John had given us, letting my eyes wander to the next chapter of Mark where I had been studying the last two days. It was verse 24 that had really caught my eye: "Therefore I tell you, whatever you ask for in prayer, believe that you have received it, and it will be yours." I read it over again and then raised my hand to speak.

"Is God really asking that question, to every one of us, right now?"

John smiled. I saw he was glad someone was paying attention. "Yes, I believe He is."

"Do you think I could ask God for healing just like Bartimaeus did? I mean, does God still act like that today?"

John paused, thrown off guard by my question. The other students in the room stared at me. I ignored their discomfort and kept going with my line of questioning. I wanted answers and I was seizing the opportunity to get them.

"You can ask God for whatever you want, Jenny, but the way He answers depends on the will of God for your life."

"What about what it says a little later in Mark chapter 11? It says that even if we ask a mountain to be thrown into the sea that it will and that if we pray for the things we want and don't doubt that God is going to give them to us, He will, so can I just ask Him for healing and expect it to happen?" I waited there in my seat, my eyes glued on John, demanding an answer.

"You read the *Bible*!?" I heard a boy call out from behind me. I wanted to roll my eyes in judgment. *This is church, isn't it? I just want an answer to my question.*

"Jenny, I…," John paused in exasperation. "This really isn't the place to discuss this. Why don't you and I talk about it more together during our retreat that that's coming up?"

"Ok," I nodded in disappointment. I didn't want to delay the answers to my questions, but I accepted his truce. The other kids in the youth group didn't seem as passionate about this topic as I was, so maybe John was right. Maybe youth group was not the place to bring this up.

As the days flew by, I searched the Bible, writing down scripture references and questions I had about healing to ask John. *Why do some people get healed and not others? Why don't we pray for the sick to get healed at our church? How long do I have to pray for healing before God does something? If I don't get healed is it because I don't have enough faith?* As I pondered my list of questions, my anticipation for the retreat grew!

Our youth group was going to spend a four-day weekend together at a conference in Duluth. We'd stay in a hotel with a pool and would get to eat every meal out! I was excited for the time ahead, excited to spend time with my friends away from my family, but most of all I was excited to finally have some one-on-one time with my pastor, to really sit down and discuss the burning questions that I held in my heart.

"I look forward to talking with you this weekend," John said as we passed in the hallway at the hotel.

"Me too," I answered with a smile. The days were filled with speakers and musicians who led worship services, with time in between to hang out near the pool. I was having a good time at the conference, but it seemed to me that every time John and I could have had an opportunity to talk, John was busy with someone else or going somewhere else. Finally, on Saturday afternoon, I lingered in the hotel lobby while the rest of the girls went shopping, hoping for an opportunity to talk to John. I had my Bible and notebook ready. "We should talk sometime today," I offered while sitting at a plastic table near the pool.

"Yeah, we should," he answered and then turned his attention to the guys who were about to start a volleyball game. Unsure of what to do with myself or how to interpret John's actions, I walked over to the hotel's exercise room and started peddling a stationary bike. As I slowly built my momentum, I also slowly realized that my long-awaited conversation with John was never going to happen, not this weekend, not ever. It wasn't because the weekend was too packed or that the demands on John's attention were stretched too thin. The reason that I would never have an opportunity to talk to John about my desire for and questions about healing was that John simply did not want to talk about it. Maybe he didn't have answers to my questions; maybe he didn't want to hear what I had to say. Whatever the reason, the result was the same: I was deeply disappointed. I had hoped that John would be the person who would come alongside me with the answers, perspective, and encouragement that I needed. I had hoped he would be the one to tell me that it was okay to ask God for healing and to hope that He would actually do it. Maybe, even though it might hurt to hear it, if it was the truth, I was hoping that John would be someone who would have the honesty to tell me not to travel down this road believing God for healing. If there was no chance God was going to heal me, then maybe I shouldn't bother. If that was the case, I should find a way to move forward and accept myself for the way I was… and therein lay a huge issue. Did I really need to accept myself for who I was?

I stared down at my thighs as they moved up and down, pumping the pedals on the bike, thinking about my body and the way that it moved. I had been taught my whole life that there was no cure for cerebral palsy. My parents had always told me, "You don't realize how lucky you are…." when speaking about the severity of my condition. CP affected each person so differently. Some people used wheelchairs, walkers, and braces in order to move around; others had slurred speech that was difficult to understand. The only difference people seemed to notice about me was the way I walked. In fact, many people didn't realize I even had a disability. Often I would hear people ask if I had been in a car accident or was recovering from an injury. The truth was, I was grateful to be alive, grateful for my abilities, but that didn't mean life was never challenging because of the *mildness* of my condition.

My mind flashed back to fifth grade physical education. We all had to go swimming together in the high school pool, except I couldn't swim. I'd never had the coordination to move my arms and legs together in rhythm, and for some reason, I always sank. I didn't want to reveal my inability to my classmates, and as the swimming unit grew closer, I felt more and more anxious about being put on display. *What would my classmates say? How would they react when they found out I couldn't swim?* I finally broke down the night before swimming started, sobbing intensely in my dad's arms as he held me close and let me cry.

Along with swimming, there were so many physical activities that I longed to do just once. Just once I wanted to wear red high heels for an evening without losing my balance. Just once I wanted to walk with a perfect gait and feel what it was like to have loose muscles. I wanted to run up bleachers and stairs independent of railings while carrying things in my hands, kick really high, and run without limitation and fatigue. Just once I wanted to play competitively in a basketball game, ride a two-wheeled bike, and water ski. Yes, my condition was mild compared to other people, but that didn't make it any less painful.

The biggest hurdle, however, of living with a disability was not physical, it was emotional. I remembered one particular morning in early elementary school when I stepped outside of the girls' bathroom to wash my hands in the sink. The sinks in the school were large stone troughs that reminded me of a bath tub with water that sprinkled out so that many people could wash their hands at once.

The sinks looked out of place to me, partly because of their large size compared to those at home but also because of their purpose. Using the bathroom was a private activity; the fact that every trip to the bathroom ended by bringing several people together to talk and wash their hands seemed funny to me.

Maybe it wasn't the sink that was out of place. Maybe it was having the opportunity to talk to other students that felt different. I had grown used to being alone as a kid at school because of my disability, being left out and left behind because of the slowness at which I moved, and yet, at the same time, I was hungry, starving even, for friendship.

One day, while I was standing at the bathroom sink washing my hands, a girl I had seen on the playground said hello to me. I had noticed her outside while I was playing because she was Korean like my cousin who was adopted and brought to the United States when he was only a few months old. I wanted to tell her about him and ask her if she too had been adopted as a baby. "Hello!" I answered back, eyes wide, smiling big.

"Can I ask you a personal question?" She looked right at me with her beautiful brown eyes as I nodded and grabbed a paper towel to dry my hands. Suddenly my hope of having the conversation I was looking forward to popped like a balloon and disappeared. This girl did not want to be my friend; I wasn't going to get to tell her about my cousin because all she wanted to know about were my legs. My heart began to fill with aching pain. Was this all anyone was ever going to see? Was this the only thing about me that my classmates would find interesting? I wanted so much to tell this girl a joke to show her that I was funny or ask her to come to my house for a sleepover or show her my new pink Skip-It that I liked to play with on the playground. Instead, I felt that I had to be polite and answer her very personal question, pretending it didn't hurt me. I knew what was coming next because I had been asked this question many times before.

"Why do you walk funny?"

Nobody understands when I give them an answer, but here goes… "I have cerebral palsy. I was born with it. I always walk this way."

She turned her head and looked at me with even more curiosity. "Does it hurt?"

"No." I shrugged my shoulders. "The funny thing is, I don't notice that I'm limping. When I walk, it feels normal to me."

She nodded, satisfied with my response, and walked back to her class. We never really spoke again. I was victim once again to an uneven exchange. She had gotten an answer to her question, and I was left exposed and alone.

I felt similar, familiar feelings that morning as I sat on the bike pedaling. I had offered my questions to someone who I thought could help and they had gone unanswered. Instead of someone walking alongside me, I was being left alone. As I slowed the pedals, I decided that if John wasn't going to show me how to continue on my journey or gently tell me to quit, then I would go at this without his help. I didn't know if it was God's will to heal me or not, but if John was right, if God still approached us today asking what He could do for us, then here was my answer: I wanted to stop having a reason to cry over the thought of being made a spectacle in physical education. I wanted to never have to answer a "personal question" again just to satisfy someone's curiosity about the way I walked. I wanted CP to become something I only had to deal with for a brief moment in childhood and only remember it as an adult. I wanted to hang on to the hope that somehow my diagnosis no longer had to hang over me like a life sentence. Somehow, hoping that God would heal me gave me a sense of power and control. I didn't have to accept that my body was different and awkward; I could instead embrace the hope that my body would eventually be sleek and perfect. How I was actually going to transform from one state to another, I was uncertain. The only thing I was certain about was that I needed answers to my questions—to help guide me on my journey. Since my youth pastor wasn't interested in walking with me, it appeared that my options were limited. I would do what I had always done when I had a question—read a book. If John didn't have the answers, surely there was someone who did.

Chapter 3

My room growing up was designed for a book lover. A wallpaper border lined the ceiling depicting various books nestled alongside antique spectacles. Every corner of my small room was optimized to contain books. My father built a floor-to-ceiling bookcase painted in white enamel. A small white desktop connected to the shelves, where I would sit on an antique chair my mother had restored to read books, do homework, and dream of the future. As I began seventh grade, questions often roamed through my mind: What will high school be like? What will I look like when I look in the mirror as an adult? What will I be when I grow up?

My room had always been my hideout, a place of quiet refuge after a lonely day at school, an escape from my brother when we would spat, a country all my own to rule with quiet thought in a house whose kingdom contained four people and a large dog. After meeting Ian Parker and being ignored by my youth pastor, I was glued to the pink cushion that sat atop my white antique chair. It was in this position that I sat hour after hour pondering the mysteries of healing as I turned the pages of my Bible along with several books on this subject. I searched for an explanation of how I could be healed of cerebral palsy like a kid on an Easter egg hunt looking for treasure, like the widow in the Bible frantically searching her house for a lost coin, like a highly motivated student cramming for the test of her life. Every time I visited a Christian bookstore, I headed straight to the section on healing; every time I heard a sermon, I hoped that the topic would be on miracles and healing; every spare minute I had, I spent searching, listening, praying.

And yet, as passionately as I pursued answers, my family were the only ones who knew of my search. Occasionally I would ask them to buy me a book, but we seldom talked together about what I was actually reading in them. I rarely let my parents into my thoughts because I wanted to keep my search as private as possible. Even worse, what if my peers at school found out what I was reading? Surely they would think I was crazy. No one would understand, but there were precious moments to read at school, time given every day in English class. One day, I decided to bring my latest pick to school, *Joni* by Joni Eareckson Tada.

Joni was the victim of a tragic diving accident in 1967 which left her paralyzed. Her recovery from this accident, it seemed to me, was a fate worse than death. Holes had to be drilled into her skull to keep her neck stabilized while she lay in an immobilizing frame, where she was flipped throughout the day to prevent bedsores. She lost her appetite even when the hospital chef personally made her a steak dinner. Her hair smelled because no one would wash it. I devoured Joni's story uninterrupted until the English teacher called me to her desk.

"What are you reading today, Jenny? You always read such a variety of books," Mrs. George asked as she looked up at me.

"I'm reading a book called *Joni*," I answered, placing the tattered book on her desk. I was pretty sure that my copy had been sitting in my parents' den since it was first published decades ago. Flowery print announced the title above an outdated photograph of Joni on the cover.

"*Joni?*" Mrs. George asked, turning her head in curiosity, "What's it about?"

Usually a bubbling fount of information on my current read, I found myself struggling with everything I had to keep the faucet turned off. If she asked me why I was reading *Joni*, I would have to tell her the truth: I was terrified that I would end up like her—disabled forever.

"It's about a girl who breaks her neck in a diving accident," I replied. "The doctors have to drill holes in her head so she can recover."

Mrs. George winced, "That sounds painful."

I nodded, agreeing. "She becomes a quadriplegic and spends the rest of her life in a wheelchair."

"Sounds like a good story. You are the genre queen, always reading something new. Keep it up!"

Happy that my secret was still safe, I walked back to my desk and continued to read. I read *Joni* during the bus ride home and all throughout the weekend, even in the morning before church. The only sight I had of the world around me was through the edges of the book. I was sucked in by her vivid depictions of her injury, feeling as though I too had broken my neck. I was terrified and captivated all at the same time. What haunted me perhaps more than the trauma of this book was Joni's perspective toward healing. Near the end of her story, Joni told how she had come to terms with God's choice not to heal her. "I would rather be in this chair knowing Him, than on my feet without Him. And that's the truth, I have no regrets, absolutely none…everything else, everything worldly pales in comparison."

That can't be true, I thought as I read Joni's words. *No one prefers to be disabled… for any reason.* I began to squirm.

I don't prefer to have cerebral palsy, even if it is for the glory of God. I hate it. My thoughts grew louder, with more anger and intensity. *I don't want to have it any more.* I stood up, as if I was lecturing Joni herself. My heart began to pound as my thoughts rushed through my mind. Nothing *compares to being able to go out for a sport, Joni, instead of having to watch your friends have all the fun.* I watched my fist clench as my index finger extended into a point. *Nothing compares to never having someone say to you "Can I ask you a personal question?" Ever again!* My breathing became heavy as tears filled my eyes. *And finally, nothing compares to not having to stare down at my scarred, spastic legs and mismatched, callused feet ever again wondering why in the world God could make them so ugly and such a visible reminder of my lack of faith. I am not going to be like you! I am not going to be disabled for the rest of my life! I am going to find a way for God to heal me!* With that, I threw the book face down under my bed. I never wanted to see a picture of Joni Erackson Tada again in my life. Her story would never have a place on my bookshelf.

A few months later, I reached under the bed, closed my eyes, and placed *Joni* into a brown paper bag. Quick as could be, I closed it tight before I could see her picture on the cover. I brought the bag out to the trash and never saw it again. A book that was supposed to offer hope and encouragement had left me doubtful and discouraged. I didn't want to read another book about accepting myself for who I was; I wanted a book that gave me answers. It was time to expand beyond my own bookshelf.

My dad not only designed and built the bookcase in my room, but he also built the bookcase in his den. Similar in style, it rose from four feet off the floor all the way to the ceiling on one side of his study. I would often sit in his pivoting desk chair and turn towards the bookshelf. It was like gazing through the glass at brightly wrapped candy in a store: antique primers from the early 1900s, reference books of every kind, parenting books (those were on the top shelf), and a plethora of fiction material. I had turned to their bookshelf before when wanting an answer to a question, so I was confident that it might once again provide the help I needed.

I stood on my dad's desk chair and peered across the shelf, looking at titles as I read the spines from left to right. I perused a few rows until I found something of interest: *Divine Healing: God's Recipe for Health and Healing* by Norvel Hays. Yes, of course! This was the book I had seen Dad reading around the house, the one a friend had recently given him. I turned the book over. It read: *This book shows you how to receive healing that is already yours. It's up to you to find out what God promises in His word so you can take hold of His healing power by faith.* This seemed like exactly the type of book I was looking for. I took it up to my bedroom and began to read.

The book started off by suggesting that if I wanted to receive healing, then I had to determine in my mind that it was actually going to happen! The author suggested that I daily say out loud things like "I am healed in Jesus name, Amen!" This idea sounded funny to me, almost like I was practicing denial. I wasn't sure how saying the opposite of what was actually happening in my body was going to help my situation, but I was desperate. Maybe, if I said it loud enough, I would eventually believe it would happen. To remind me to say these statements on a daily basis, I took out the white Ed Emberly drawing pad my grandma gave me for Christmas and a pink highlighter and began to make posters and tape them to the outside of my closet door. I wrote things like: *You can have what you ask for in prayer, Mark 11:24; By His Stripes I am Healed; and My Healing will Manifest* (I wasn't even sure what the word meant, but I had read about it over and over again in the book, so I thought it was a good idea to include it).

Every morning, I woke up and stared at my pink posters. I read them over and over, said their phrases aloud until they blended into the background of my room. Looking at them became routine until one day when I had my friend Lizzy over. Lizzy and I had been friends for a few years and she was coming over to hang out. We got to my room midway through a conversation when she stopped talking and just stared at my closet door. I could see her mouth moving as she took in what was written on every poster. I stood behind her, mortified, powerless to stop her. My journey towards healing was supposed to be a secret! None one could possibly understand what I was doing; I hardly understood what I was doing…I hadn't finished reading the book yet. Lizzy turned around with a confused look on her face and said nothing. I could tell she thought I was crazy. I said nothing in return. When Lizzy went home, I tore the posters down and threw them in the same trash bin where *Joni* had landed months ago. "Claiming" my healing was not working; it was time to look directly in the Bible for answers.

Perhaps prayer was the key that would someday unlock the door to my healing. I was always taught in Sunday school that Jesus said, "I tell you the truth, if you have faith as small as a mustard seed, you can say to this mountain, 'Move from here to there' and it will move. Nothing will be impossible for you." I had seen mustard seeds while looking in my mother's spice cabinet. They were minuscule—hardly bigger than the colored sprinkles that dotted the tops of cupcakes. I had faith that size; in fact, after reading Norvel Hay's book, my faith became poster-sized (except when Lizzy came over).

But, if I did have faith, and I had asked, commanded even, that my mountain of CP go drown itself, why had nothing happened? It was this question that became the topic of family conversation during the car ride home one Sunday after church.

"How much faith is enough faith for God to perform a miracle?" I asked aloud from the passenger-side captain's chair in the middle of our family's van.

"Well, Jenny," my dad began to answer, making eye contact through the rearview mirror, "The Bible says that if you have faith the size of a mustard seed— "

"I know that, *Dad*," I interjected, almost interrupting as I leaned farther forward in my seat. "But how much is *enough*? How do you know when your faith is *big enough* for God to act?"

My mother sat in the passenger's seat, silent and listening. This time, surprisingly, it was my brother Gabe who spoke.

"I don't think it's about having a certain amount," he said matter-of-factly. "I think that passage is saying you either have faith or you don't."

"Yeah. I think that's right, Gabe," my father responded, nodding. "That's a better way of putting it."

I sat across from my brother, speechless. What he said I had never considered before. If he was right, then I was sunk. I had faith, I was sure of it, and it was bigger than a cupcake sprinkle. Even scarier, if I had faith, why hadn't I seen anything happen?

I continued to ponder this thought throughout the summer and into the fall of my eighth grade year when my mother showed me a newspaper ad—Ian Parker was back in town.

Chapter 4

$\mathcal{I}$ walked into the auditorium with both of my parents and we took our seats somewhere towards the back. The meeting had started about 45 minutes earlier and there were still musicians up on stage. Some of the songs were ones I was familiar with, but others were clearly written in England and had yet to make their way to the United States. This made an activity I usually enjoyed hard to participate in, but I tried to sing along, echoing choruses whose lyrics were flashing on an overhead screen.

After the music finished, an offering was taken, and then Ian began to preach. He talked about how the Holy Spirit lives inside us and, because of this, we can use the Spirit's power to minister to others, doing all kinds of miraculous things like casting out demons, healing the sick, and raising the dead. Ian was the only person I had ever heard speak of such works being carried out in modern day. I would love to be healed of my condition, but the thought of casting out a demon or raising a dead person both intrigued and frightened me. God did these things in the Bible, so it must be okay…right?

After he had finished preaching, Ian moved on to his initial altar call. Unlike a Billy Graham crusade where some people in the crowd come forward at the end of a sermon, *everyone* rose from their seats and moved towards the stage for prayer. I looked towards my parents, unsure what to do next. I had never seen a whole group of people come forward at the end of a sermon—usually on a Sunday, people did the reverse and headed towards the door, hungry for lunch and wanting to talk with their friends. My dad looked at me and motioned, "Go ahead," so I followed the crowd in front of me towards the stage.

As I returned to the stage, I was flooded with images from a year ago: being pulled out of bed in confusion, bright lights shining down on me as a mysterious person prayed for me. But this year was different. I wasn't confused, I was desperate. More than anything, I wanted to be healed and I had come that night only for that reason. I felt like the bleeding woman in the Bible who had spent all her money on doctors and treatments, desperately trying to find a cure. In her desperation, she reached out to Jesus for healing, knowing that He was her final and only hope. Tonight, I was going to reach out to Ian. I had read my Bible, prayed my prayers, and nothing had happened. I was not going to end up like Joni and merely accept my disability for the rest of my life! I had faith that God was going to heal me—I just needed someone to help it happen.

Just then, my thoughts were interrupted by an assistant who was organizing people into rows so that everyone had enough space. I became separated from my parents but was too consumed with my thoughts to pay any attention. I sat down quietly on stage among strangers and waited. Ian soon walked by and prayed for the woman sitting next to me. When he was finished, I reached out my hand and touched him. He looked at me, distracted, and moved on to pray for someone else. I retracted my hand, disappointed. Maybe reaching out to him was the wrong thing to do. Unlike the woman in the Bible, I was not instantly healed by reaching out my hand and my gesture did not cause Ian to stop what he was doing in order to find out "who had touched him." Even though my plan had failed, I was not ready to give up. I continued to wait there silently; perhaps he would return. Five minutes later, he did!

Ian knelt down beside me, put his hand on my shoulder, looked me straight in the eye, and said, "You reached out and touched me earlier. What do you need prayer for?"

My eyes filled with hope! I held my breath for a moment, realizing that perhaps I was going to get an opportunity tonight to make my request after all. I let out a breath and with boldness I answered, "I would like to be healed of cerebral palsy."

Ian paused, blinking, taking in my answer to his question. He spoke into his headset microphone and gently confirmed, "You have cerebral palsy?" I nodded silently, and looked into his eyes, hoping he would know what to do.

"Just stand up right here." Ian reached out his hand and helped me to my feet. I stood on stage, once again for all to see. Although I could feel the eyes of the audience staring at me, I shut them out by closing my eyes. I may have been on stage, but in many ways this was a private moment between a girl and her God. I knew God had seen my desire, and here I was, simply holding my heart out before Him. *Will you heal me tonight God, please? I'll do anything! I just don't want to have CP anymore.* I bowed my head and waited.

Ian began to pray. "Father, in the name of Jesus Christ, I ask you to heal my sister of cerebral palsy. I'm going to lay my hands on you and I want you to just receive this free gift from God." As Ian laid his hands on my shoulders, I stood there, listening, hoping something would happen. Perhaps I would feel it in my mind first, or would it be my legs? As much as I wanted healing to happen instantly, I tried to be patient; perhaps that's what Ian meant when he told me to "just receive" from God.

Unfortunately, even though I followed Ian's directions the best I could, the only thing that happened was that I began to tremble. Soon I could no longer stand and fell to the floor where someone quickly wrapped me once again in a blanket. This evening seemed to be a repeat of what had happened a year ago. I lay there on the floor, shaking and confused. I realized in that moment that I didn't know any more about how to "be healed" than I knew how to raise a dead person or cast out a demon. What I was asking from God was beyond my understanding. Unlike a year ago, God did not seem near to me as I lay on stage, staring at the lights; God felt distant. I had just cried out to Him in my silence and I found the absence of His answer to my plea deafening.

"Ian, why wasn't I healed tonight?" The meeting had closed, but my parents and I had stayed behind to talk to Ian in the back of the auditorium as people filtered out. My dad had reintroduced us, and a year later, Ian had remembered me.

"I don't know why some people are healed and others have to wait," Ian answered honestly, addressing all three of us. "Sometimes persistence in prayer is key." He paused for a second, nodding and then pointed at me. "You need to be prayed for every day until something changes and I would like you to keep coming to my meetings."

I looked at my dad, silently asking for permission. He nodded reassuringly.

"Ok," I said with a timid smile.

"Good. I believe God is going to heal you, Jenny," Ian stared into my eyes, affirming my deepest hope. "You just need to be expectant and seek Him."

I left the auditorium light-headed and reeling. "God is going to heal me, God is going to heal me," I repeated to myself over and over again. I let Ian's words permanently map themselves onto my brain as I looked out the window during the car ride home.

The next evening I returned to Ian's meeting with my parents. We took our place near the back; I had brought my Bible with me as well as a notebook and pen. This time, I had no plans to doodle. I found myself fully aware, hanging on every word that Ian had to say, hoping that he could somehow bring about my healing.

"Sometimes people don't experience healing because of sin in their life," Ian began. What sin could I have possibly committed that was keeping me from my healing? I couldn't think of anything, but maybe I had committed a sin that I just couldn't remember and had never asked for forgiveness.

"Sometimes people don't get healed because of corporate unbelief," he continued. *Corporate unbelief?* I asked myself, confused. The only time I had ever heard the word "corporate" was when someone was talking about a corporation, and I was sure that businesses had nothing to do with healing. I tugged on my dad's sleeve and whispered, "What is he talking about?"

"Corporate unbelief is when the whole church doesn't believe, so then miracles don't take place. Jesus talks about in the New Testament how He couldn't perform any miracles because of people's lack of faith."

"Oh," I whispered back, nodding. If it was other people's faith that was preventing my miracle, I didn't see how it was possible to make other people believe or care if I went home healed or not. I had spent the last year trying to focus my brain and believe that God was going to heal me despite the fact that I woke each morning to stare down at my scarred, stiff legs. I had quit using the phrase "cerebral palsy" and often tried to pretend I didn't have CP just so I could focus on the fact that someday it would be true. It seemed to be taking everything I had to privately believe I was going to be healed—how could the church as a whole possibly muster up enough faith to believe for me as well?

"And some people don't receive their healing because of a Spirit of Infirmity."

Spirit of Infirmity? Was Ian talking about demons?

"Open your Bibles to Luke 13, verse 10."

Obediently, I opened my Bible and began to follow along with Ian:

On a Sabbath Jesus was teaching in one of the synagogues, and a woman was there who had been crippled by a spirit for eighteen years. She was bent over and could not straighten up at all. When Jesus saw her, he called her forward and said to her, "Woman, you are set free from your infirmity." Then he put his hands on her, and immediately she straightened up and praised God.

"Sometimes, people have a spirit inside them that they need to be delivered from in order to receive their healing, just like this woman. Jesus set her free and 'she straightened up and praised God.'"

I sat in my seat, listening to Ian, hoping that my absence of a miracle fell into this third category, that the reason I wasn't seeing healing in my life had nothing to do with my personal sin or someone else's lack of faith that would surely never be buoyed. If my problem was demonic, all that needed to happen was someone needed to pray for me to have this "spirit" removed and then I could be instantly healed…right? I wasn't sure what being delivered entailed, but I was willing to try anything.

"Where's Jenny?"

I looked up to meet Ian's gaze, surprised to hear the sound of my name being called from the stage.

"I'm right here!" I called out, excited that this might be my moment!

"Come up here, Jenny, I want to pray for you."

I ran to the front and up the stairs as fast as I could. My heart was beating rapidly and a smile was growing wider across my face...this was it!

"Stand right here in front of me; I'm going to pray for you." Ian turned and faced the crowd. "I want the rest of you to extend your hands and pray for Jenny." I watched as hundreds of people, their eyes glued on me, stretched out their arms and hands as if wanting to touch me. I was glad for their encouragement but scared at how many people were watching. This discomfort was complicated by my growing excitement. My healing was just moments away!

I bowed my head, locking my eyes shut, trying to block out the publicity of the moment.

"Father, in the name of Jesus Christ, I ask you to heal Jenny, right now!" Whoosh! Ian blew into his headset microphone once again like he was trying to pass the power of his prayers on to me. I stood there in front of him, concentrating with all my might, trying to "receive" the healing that I had been asking for.

Ian continued to pray, "Spirit of Infirmity, I command you to be loosed from this body in Jesus' name. Be loosed from her, you foul, nasty thing!"

In a whirlwind of emotion, time seemed to spin around me and yet pause at the same time. Unexpectedly, my thoughts changed from hopeful and excited to discouraged and confused. Foul and nasty? Those words weren't in the verses we read this evening. Did I really just hear this man pray those words over me in front of a crowd? Was I foul and nasty, or was he talking about my cerebral palsy? If he meant my cerebral palsy, did that mean that people who had CP were foul and nasty too? And what if I couldn't get rid of my foul and nasty condition? Did that mean I would be a disgusting, sinful failure for the rest of my life? Why was it not okay to have a disability? I never thought it personally meant I was not okay as a human being; I just didn't like it...I couldn't help the way I was born and I couldn't make God change it, but if He thought I was foul and nasty than I had better do something about it. I had better try really hard to make sure that this "spirit" left me.

With full control of my body, will, and emotions, I made two conscious decisions. One, I would surrender myself fully into the sensation of the moment and react whatever way necessary, no matter how foolish, in order to be "delivered." Two, I would distance myself from my own body, making a conscious separation between my mind and spirit, and my physical self that was just named foul and nasty, desperately needing to be changed from the way it was. In that moment, I began to think that having CP was a shameful, horrible, public display that I was doomed to carry around proclaiming that I was spiritually deficient. I had a moral obligation to rid myself of this condition, to surrender to this man's instructions, if I was ever going to have a chance of ridding myself of my "scarlet letter" and one day become a whole person.

Snapping out of my thoughts and back into reality, I let myself fall to the ground as Ian continued to pray. As if trying to break a spell that had been cast over me, I began to hear Ian proclaim into his microphone: "It breaks! It breaks!"

What "breaks?" I thought, struggling to comprehend Ian's prayers. Almost on cue, I began to whip my head back and forth on the floor screaming in fits of rage. I wanted this thing out of me too! I began to kick my legs, tightening all of my muscles in my body, using all my strength in attempt to free myself as Ian was commanding. I kept struggling, kicking, screaming, grunting, and willing my body to transform. In the midst of my madness, I realized something frightening and terrible was happening around me. Ian had stopped praying just to watch me move, along with the rest of the crowd.

Everyone was now watching me, poised in silence. *How could this be happening?* I started to think in the midst of my outburst. This was supposed to be a private war between me and God. Why was I on stage? I shouldn't be here. This shouldn't be happening. I shouldn't be acting like this; it's foolish.

I have to act foolishly, I negotiated with myself as I breathed in, summoning enough energy to continue, *I have to ignore the crowd and let myself be delivered. I have to forget about how horrible I am acting right now in order to let my healing happen. I can't have CP forever; it shows my sin, my lack of faith, my failure.* Suddenly, I heard Ian's voice again, encouraging me on as my legs began to shake. "This leg is straightening out; one used to be longer than the other, now they're the same length."

Why are you announcing that to the crowd? I wanted to call out and make him stop. Nothing was happening to my legs at that moment other than a severe muscle spasm. They weren't growing; my body felt no different.

"That's it, just let healing come. Just receive, Jenny."

I laid there on the floor and tried to "receive" my healing, but it was not coming and I was growing exhausted. As my energy began to wane, I slowed down, quieted, opened my eyes, and took in the scene around me. Lights were again glaring down on my face. I turned to the side. My mom was sitting beside me. *When did she get here?* I thought. As I continued to look around, I noticed that the whole meeting had stopped and several people were gathered around me, more were standing off the stage looking on.

"I'm thirsty," I told my mom.

"She needs some water!" I heard someone in the crowd call.

Very quickly a plastic cup holding cool water was handed to me and I began to sip, taking in the refreshment. A few minutes later, a woman gave me an energy bar. I ate it as if I were starving and hadn't eaten in days.

"Can you get up?" Ian's British accent interrupted my munching and I nodded. My mom helped me to my feet. "Can you walk around? Do you notice anything different?" I started to walk around the stage, bending and flexing my legs. I shook my head in silence. No.

"We'll just keep praying for you, Jenny, and believing." Ian turned to the crowd, "Let's give the Lord a clap offering." The crowd applauded, and while I was grateful to have people with me in my journey, I was exhausted and discouraged. More than anything I wanted to go home and sleep. I wanted to escape this moment where people were cheering for unfinished work. I needed to rest so that I could regain my strength and continue this marathon of faith again tomorrow. It was if I was running on a treadmill, working hard, but ultimately going nowhere. I couldn't see my destination, but I knew I had to keep working if healing was ever going to happen.

Chapter 5

The room that held the pool felt humid and steamy as I stood near the water's edge. Last night's "exorcism" had been unsuccessful, so Ian had suggested that I try baptism tonight just in case "there was anything standing between me and God that might hinder my miracle." I wasn't sure why I needed to be baptized…again. My dad had already baptized me in Eagle Lake several years ago and I had never heard of anyone being baptized twice, but if Ian thought it would help me, then of course I would do it!

I looked down into the water at the two men in the pool waiting to baptize me on Ian's command. Slowly, I turned around and entered the water, lowering myself into the pool using a ladder. The water was cold and I could feel my muscles growing rigid as the waves lapped my skin. I watched as Ian extended his hand from the pool deck and prayed, "Jenny, I baptize you in the name of the Father, the Son, and the Holy Spirit." I closed my eyes and plugged my nose as the water encompassed me. When I came up, I began to thrash around, kicking and screaming much like the night before when Ian prayed for me on stage.

I could have stopped. I could have composed myself, letting my body relax, gently allowing myself to glide across the pool. But, just like the night before, I gave myself permission to express all of the emotion that was inside of me. Maybe if I exerted more energy, gave this more effort, God would see how hard I was working and heal me. I contracted my stomach muscles, clenched my teeth, and moaned while the men struggled to grab hold and escort me to the other side of the pool to where my mother was sitting. Once on the deck, I sat on a towel and howled near the top of my lungs for the rest of the evening.

While sitting there crying, I intermittently looked around the room at who was there and how they were reacting. Some of the people standing around the pool were people I recognized. Others were strangers who were staring at me. I imagined their thoughts as I sat there: "Shut up! You're interrupting the whole meeting! What are you *doing?*" *I must look awful.* My hair was sopping wet, tangled, and messy from my trip into the water, my body was contorting in twisted and unnatural movements as I sat there struggling, and my mouth was endlessly letting out screams and moans piercing the atmosphere.

I raised my left hand up, like I had seen other people do while singing songs during worship. In the midst of my howling, I still wanted to remain open, I wanted to "receive" from God. I was also raising my hand because I wanted attention. I wanted attention from Ian. I wanted him to stop praying for other people, and pray for me exclusively like he had the night before. I wasn't healed yet; his work wasn't done. I needed him to pray for me because he seemed to be the only one with the answers.

I also wanted attention from God. Didn't He see me down here, desperately hoping for a miracle, hoping that tonight I would walk home free from CP, free from my shame? My howling cries that rose from the depths of my gut were as much about making noise as they were cries of grief and sorrow. It was as if my whole being ached for a different outcome than the one being orchestrated. Every cry, every moan, every writhing movement I was making was my grieving, wounded spirit. *Don't You hear me, God? Don't You see how bad I want this? Everyone else is staring at me, why can't You just take minute to look at me? God, are You there…*

These questions continued to cramp my mind, overwhelming my consciousness, for the next five months as praying for healing became the sole focus of my life. I was prayed for almost every night, either at home by my father or by Ian himself when my parents would take me to his meetings. I stood in front for prayer, hoping every night that this was the night that God was going to heal me and left each meeting discouraged. In the morning, I would wake up, rip back my comforter, and stare down at my legs. Were they straight? Did God heal me overnight in my sleep? Often, I would close my eyes and picture what my new legs would look like once God healed me. My knee would no longer turn in, and my left foot would look identical to my right. I dreamed of standing on a stage, just like Ian, declaring what God had done in my life. The scars from my surgery would be erased, and I would stand perfectly straight. This process of "prayer," "peek," and "picture" repeated night after night as my hopes were raised and smashed like tidal waves breaking against the rocks.

"Jenny, we've invited the pastor and his wife over here to pray for you this evening," my dad explained as I sat in our living room with my parents, staring across the couch at a couple I had hardly met. We had recently decided to attend the local church that was sponsoring Ian's visit instead of the church I had grown up in. This one believed in healing.

My mother brought a chair from the kitchen table and set it in the center of the room. "Why don't you go ahead and have a seat," my pastor said as he gestured towards the chair. As I sat there, I bowed my head and set my teeth. Prayer had become a painful experience.

The other four sat around me, their heads bowed and eyes closed. I heard the pastor's wife pray first.

"Father, we thank you for this precious life. We thank you for the work you are doing in her. Lord, in the name of Jesus, we ask that you would heal her from cerebral palsy." I felt a hand placed upon my back. I sat there in silence. Nothing happened. After a while, I opened my eyes and sat up.

My dad had pulled out his Bible. "I want to read this passage to you, Jenny. It's the one you recite all the time, Mark 11:24: 'Therefore I tell you, whatever you ask for in prayer, believe that you have received it, and it will be yours.'"

Hearing my dad read about faith when I had prayed and believed for so long felt like mockery. In a fit of rage and frustration, I looked at him and screamed, "I hate this book!" and before he could stop me, I reached out my hand and tore the page clear out of his Bible.

He stopped, looked up at me in surprise, but didn't say anything in response. I couldn't believe what I had just done. Out of all the things I had allowed myself to do in the past several months, this act shocked me the most. I began to weep.

It started softly at first. My eyes started to fill with water and tears spilled down my cheeks. My shoulders started to heave, and then I began to crumple. My sobs grew louder and louder as I struggled to breathe. I fell off the chair, curled up in the fetal position in the corner of the living room and wailed.

My mom came over and put her hand on my back, trying to comfort me. I just ignored it and kept weeping. Over the sounds of my sobbing, I heard my pastor quietly ask my dad, "Is this how your prayer times usually end?"

There was silence for a minute and then my dad replied, "She's never broken down like this before."

I could tell by the sound of confusion in his voice that my parents didn't know what to make of my behavior, so uncharacteristic of how I had acted so many times before. I, however, felt like I finally had a moment of clarity as I lay on the living room floor. I had been running hard after healing, exerting everything I had, and even though I hadn't reached my destination, it was time to step down from the treadmill and go speak to the Trainer. His plan wasn't working and I was one unsatisfied customer.

Chapter 6

The house that I grew up in lay next to a potato field just across a country road from my backyard. I would go there often to walk my dog Brutus, a 75-pound German Shepherd Collie mutt, down the dirt path that separated rows of crops. This was Brutus' favorite place to walk as well because it meant that he didn't have to be on a leash. We'd walk across the backyard, cross the county road together, and then I would give him the signal. "Go ahead!" I would nod.

He would look at me with his tongue hanging out of his mouth and his tail spinning. Then, he would take off romping. I often wouldn't see him again until it was time to cross the road to go home, but while I walked, I would see a tail sticking up somewhere in the dirt. His nose, I knew, was close to the ground, sniffing for animals. It was in these fields where I walked each day that I gained space to spend time alone. It was also in these fields where I grieved the loss of my dreams.

Having given up my running shoes the night before, I walked into the field that day to do business: I needed to confront God. At first, I had no words. I just felt the weight of heavy pain inside my chest. It clutched my heart so tightly my voice became strangled. I tried to form words, tried to move my lips, but all I could do was weep. Then, gradually, the words came.

"How could You?" I demanded. "How could You look down at me and decide not to heal me after I had asked so many times?" I paused, taking a few steps, stamping my feet and pumping my arms in an angry stride. "I hate my body. I hate the fact that I have to wake up every morning staring at legs and feet that remind me so brutally of my failure." I stopped talking for a moment, hoping the heavens would answer back.

"You!" I belted out, pointing an accusing finger towards the sky. "You're supposed to 'be the same yesterday, today, and forever,' right?" I began to breathe heavily. "I thought You were *not a respecter of persons*," I hissed. "I didn't even know what 'respecter of persons' meant before this whole thing started. But lucky You," I took a deep breath, inhaling more air to continue arguing, "I've looked it up. I know what it means. It means that You are not supposed to like anyone more than anyone else." I fell silent again, waiting for a rebuttal. "So I'll ask You again," I squared my shoulders and stared up at the sky. "How could You heal other people and not heal *me*?"

"I want out of this relationship," I said the next day as Brutus and I made our trek. I felt like I was asking God for a divorce. I never imagined my most precious relationship was going to end like this, yet my desire was sincere. "I don't know who You are anymore," I felt compelled to give a reason for my request. "I don't understand how I can love You or even be *in a relationship* with You when I can't understand You." I stopped for a moment and put my hands on my hips.

"I don't understand why Your Son would come and heal the lame while He walked on the earth and endure torture for our sickness and disease, yet when I've asked You to heal me, You have done nothing." Catching my breath, I continued, "Either the Bible isn't true, or You're not who You say You are. I can't handle either reality." Hot tears streamed down my face as I stood there, heartbroken.

I walked to the end of the path and got ready to turn around. This was usually the spot where I started to compose myself because I wanted to keep my emotion secret. No one was to know of my pain. This was a private grief and all the responsibility for not being healed was only on me and God. As I began to pivot in the dirt, turning towards home, I heard a voice. Not an audible whisper, but rather words in my mind. I had heard words like these before when I walked the halls of my elementary school as a child, pouring my heart out, telling Him of my loneliness. In those moments, I heard the promise, "I will be your friend." Now, I was hearing Him again, "You can go if you want, but please don't. Please stay."

I turned around and sat in the dirt. I crossed my legs and hugged my knees as I brought them up to my chest. I ran my tongue over my teeth, considering the words that I had just heard. I didn't want to "divorce" God; deep within my heart of hearts I didn't want to turn from Him. The truth was, the very thought of continuing my life without faith was even scarier than trying to trust a God that I didn't understand. So, maybe I did have a reason to continue this relationship, even if that reason was simply fear.

"Alright," I said, standing up. "I won't leave, but here's the deal," I said, pointing at the sky. "I can't talk to You about healing any more. It hurts too much."

Chapter 7

"Jenny, I need you to look me in the eyes."

I raised my head and met the gaze of my school's physical therapist. Throughout my whole school career, she checked in with me to measure how far I could stretch my leg muscles to determine my range of motion. Now that I was starting high school, she wanted to get a feel for where I was at. Today she was not pleased with the results.

"Your condition is permanent." She raised her eye brows, staring even further into me, trying to capture more of my attention. "You're going to have cerebral palsy for the rest of your life." She paused. "Jenny, you need to stretch every day so that you can move easily. It is very important. Do you understand me?"

I nodded my head reluctantly. *If only you knew, I thought, how much of an act of betrayal it is for me to agree with you. If only I would have prayed harder, I wouldn't be sitting here right now.*

"There's another thing I think you need in addition to your daily stretching routine."

"What is it?" I asked with some surprise.

"I think you need to wear braces."

Braces!? Why did I need to wear braces? My mind raced back to my childhood when I was relearning to walk after surgery. Customized plastic molds were made so that I could wear braces up to my ankles, supporting my feet. They were hot and sweaty and so uncomfortable. But that was the least of my concerns. When I was four, I didn't care much what I looked like. Wearing braces then meant that I got to pick out a new pair of shoes because they had to be one size bigger to make room for everything. Now I cared *a lot* about the way I looked. What were my classmates going to say? I could only imagine the scene, especially if I was wearing sandals:

"What are you *wearing?*" some cute guy would inevitably ask.

"Braces," I would respond with timid shame, scared to meet his eyes.

"Why in the world do you need to wear *braces?*" he would glare down at me, demanding an answer, totally oblivious to the awkwardness of his question.

"Because I have cerebral palsy," I would quietly respond.

There would be no response to this, just some awkward look. Then he would lean down, stare harder at my feet, and react just like a girl had done one summer at camp when I had taken off my sandals while sitting in the sand.

"Eeew!" What is that on your foot? It's totally disgusting! Quick! Cover it up!"

I would probably tell the cute boy the same thing that I had told the girl. I would tell him that they were bunions, and they were on the side of my feet because of the way I walk.

What I really wanted to say was this: "I know, the fact that I have cerebral palsy is weird and I know my feet are ugly and disgusting." Then I would look him right in the eye, making sure he could understand me. "I'm *sorry* you have to look at me. You need to understand that I *tried* to ask God for healing, really I did, but I didn't have enough faith and I didn't pray hard enough." My head would start to hang as I said my final words, "I don't really know what went wrong, but all of this is my fault."

"Jenny, I'm still talking to you," the physical therapist's voice interrupted. I was more than happy to be rescued from my nightmare.

"Sorry."

"You need to see your doctor. You need to see what he thinks about this, but I think wearing braces would help keep your feet in a stable position throughout the day."

"Ok," I nodded again, "I'll make an appointment."

Two weeks later, I found myself sitting in an exam room at Gillette Children's Hospital, waiting to see my doctor. Suddenly, I saw the doorknob turn. "Jenny, good to see you! It's been a while." The renowned orthopedic surgeon from my childhood, Dr. Koop, stood before me wearing what appeared to be the same clothes he wore when I had last seen him over five years ago—a white lab coat over a dress shirt and pants and, who could forget, his signature bow tie.

He consulted his charts and then looked up, "So, you're here today to talk about braces."

"Yes," I said sighing, "The school PT thinks I need to wear them. She thinks if I keep my feet more upright, I'll be more supported throughout the day." *Please don't make me wear them; please don't make me wear them!* I silently prayed. *I'll look like a loser!*

Dr. Koop paused, pondering what I had just said. After taking a few measurements and checking my range of motion, he sat back on his stool and delivered his verdict. "I think school PTs are great, I really do," he brought his hand up to his chin before continuing to speak, "but so often they go to conferences, get all kinds of ideas about orthotics, and then I end up fielding several referrals of patients from the same school district the following week." He looked me in the eye. "It is my professional opinion that you do not need braces at this time."

Whew! I had dodged a bullet! I wouldn't have to have any awkward conversations with cute boys about strange plastic molds Velcroed to my ankles. But what if someone asked about my feet again?

"Dr. Koop, before you go, could take a look at my feet?"

Unlike the girl at summer camp, he did not look at my feet in disgust, but instead reached out and held them in his bare hands. He didn't just stare at them either. He touched them skillfully, moving my toes, rotating my feet to take in the full picture of what he was holding. He looked up at me and said, "I see this often in patients with CP. You have bunions on the side of your left foot because you walk on that side of your foot instead of the bottom," he held up my foot to illustrate his point. "I could remove them, but they will probably just form again and most patients find that the surgery does little to improve their appearance. As long as they aren't causing you any pain…"

"They aren't."

"I'll leave them alone." He sat there for a second and then looked me in the eyes and said, "Jenny, I want you to know that your feet are normal."

I sat on the exam table, unable to do anything except stare at Dr. Koop in disbelief. Did he really just say that my feet were "normal?" His words were like light trying to pierce through a cracked door into a darkened room, challenging my stubborn thoughts about my feet and my disability. I leaned back on my elbows, my mind reeling. No one had ever told me my feet were normal, especially not someone who held such authority. I let myself accept a little of what he had to say and felt a flood of warmth cascade down my body from head to feet. Maybe having cerebral palsy didn't *automatically* make me "foul and nasty," and maybe my bunions weren't so repulsive. I sat there, wishing I could bring this man to school. Every time someone made a comment about how disgusting my feet looked, this man could assure them that I was normal. They may not listen to me, but I was sure they'd listen to him—he was a surgeon.

"How can I become like Dr. Koop?" I asked my dad one evening after school.

"He's a surgeon, honey," he answered not fully understanding my question. "You'd have to go to med school."

"I know that, but that's not what I'm asking," I said, shaking my head.

"When I was with him this week, it was different."

"How so?"

"I was impressed with his intelligence, of course, but it was more than that." I paused, shaking my head, searching for words, trying to describe a quality I had never experienced before in another human being. "He was compassionate. It almost felt like I was in the presence of greatness and yet," I shrugged, "he made me feel welcome to be there. He made me feel good about myself."

My dad nodded, finally understanding. "I've felt humbled sitting in his office before too," my dad looked away, thinking, "but I don't know how you can become like him. Sorry."

I walked away, disappointed. This would have to be something to discuss with God in the potato field. I wanted to be able to see myself like Dr. Koop saw me. He was able to hold my crooked feet and see normal. All I saw were my crooked feet and my shame. If I could be like Dr. Koop, having CP wouldn't be so hard.

"Ok Brutus, ready? Go!" Brutus bolted forward into the field after school while I walked slowly behind him, picking at the tall weeds that bent forward into my path.

"God, I met a man this week that I want to model my life after. I want to be like Dr. Koop." As I walked along the path, I thought about all the hours this man must have spent studying and training to become a surgeon. He had developed his gifts in order to help people in a way that few could.

"I don't need to become an orthopedic surgeon, but I want to study hard. I want to be the best at something so that one day I can help other people too." I looked down at my legs, watching my stride as I moved along. The truth was, Dr. Koop was responsible for my gait. When I originally learned to walk, I walked with my right foot turned in and my left foot flipped over, dragging behind. I fell constantly. During my operation, Dr. Koop worked to lengthen my tendons so my feet hit the ground correctly. My femurs were broken and my legs turned out so that my walk transformed from a tangled struggle to a slight limp. What if Dr. Koop had decided not to study, not to become a surgeon? Would I even be able to do something as simple as walk in this field? I shuttered at the thought.

"I want to be compassionate; I want to be welcoming; I want to tell people they're normal," the words fell from my lips in a rush. I picked up my pace, trying to match my speed to the intensity of my words. What I was about to say next was going to take some courage.

"I need to be the best at something for another reason. I need this for me too." I tried to fight back the tears. "I can't be a failure at everything, okay?

I need something to be good at. I'll never be an athlete; my classmates *asked me to quit* marching band; I don't have many friends…." I hung my head, hunched my shoulders, and wept. The dirt slowly speckled into tiny clumps as my tears hit the ground. "I thought we had a good relationship…now that's even ruined."

I started to sniffle and reached into my pocket for a Kleenex. "I can't pray without pain. I grimace every time I open the Bible. Do you know *how hard it is* to read about Jesus healing people who were crippled?" I closed my eyes and shook my head, "I need this one, God. I need this."

Goals for High School, I wrote on a piece of notebook paper as I sat at my desk in my bedroom following my walk.

1. I will live my life with excellence and integrity.
2. I will treat school like a professional job.
3. I will complete every assignment to the absolute best of my ability.
4. I will be inducted into the National Honor Society next year.
5. I will graduate in the top 10.

I pinned the list to my bulletin board and went to sleep.

"You've been asked to come here this afternoon because you are a very special group of students. I like to call you the 'and then some' population. We ask you to do your all; you give it your 100% effort 'and then some.'"

It was near the end of my sophomore year, and I was in my high school auditorium, listening with anticipation as the Dean of Students talked about applying to the National Honor Society. My hopes of acceptance were high!

"This organization is not for 8:00-3:00ers," he explained. "We're not here to recognize students who are just here for the academics. We want to applaud the well-rounded student—those that are heavily involved in extra-curricular activities: wrestling, basketball, band, choir, yearbook…."

His speech continued on, but I stopped listening, placed my index finger near my temple, and just glared. I was so enraged that I wanted to scream at him. It took everything I had to stay glued in my seat and not storm out of the auditorium. My thoughts began to sound sassy. *We can't all be* state wrestling champions *like you, can we?* I glared at him even harder, growing more incensed.

You think athletics is just something that we can all just choose to be involved in, don't you? Well, I'll tell you what," I imagined myself up in his face, hand on my hip, index finger pointing and waving. *I did not choose to watch all of my friends enjoy sports while I sat on the sidelines. I did not choose to have my hand-eye coordination so messed up that by the time I got to high school, participating in band became overwhelming. I did not choose to have cerebral palsy. Academics are all I have. I'm sorry that I'm not well-rounded enough for you.* I imagined I would turn to walk away, pivoting around to give the final word: *You try living my life; I'm sure you wouldn't amount to more than an* 8:00-3:00er *either.*

Looking down at the National Honor Society application in my hand, I knew that I could apply, but it would only result in rejection. A week later I was notified that I had not been selected, and in a burst of anger, rage, and disappointment, I blamed my pain on my mother.

Showing her the rejection letter, I screamed, "You raised me wrong!" My mom looked down, trying to hide the tears falling from her eyes. Angry that she wouldn't meet my gaze, I pressed further. "Why didn't you tell me?!" I raised my voice and asked the question again, "Why didn't you tell me that there were going to be opportunities that I was going to be excluded from in life because I have cerebral palsy?"

I sat there, waiting for an answer. Of course I knew that athletics was never going to be an option, but the idea that I would be excluded from an academic award had taken me by surprise. I was furious and I felt like someone *owed me* an explanation. "Why didn't you tell me that I was going to be disappointed!?" I screamed and cried in a flurry of tears, angry at the situation, and devastated that I could no longer contain my pain. My mom needed to hurt like I did, otherwise I would explode.

"I'm sorry," Mom began to answer me between intermittent sobs. "We raised you the best we could. We didn't want to ever sit you down and have a conversation where we said 'Now Jenny, there are certain things you are not going to be able do because of your cerebral palsy.' We didn't want you to look at your life in terms of your limitations."

"Humpf." I turned away from my mother, my arms across my chest. Staring out the window, I hoped with everything inside me that adulthood would come quickly; I wanted my childhood to end.

Chapter 8

As much as I hoped that somehow I could push the "fast forward" button on my life's remote control and speed through my remaining years living at home, it seemed that my remote was stuck on real time. I couldn't fast forward through my junior and senior year of high school, but I could change the channel as often as possible. When the school bell rang at the end of the day, many of my friends would head to track practice but I would head home. They hit the gym, trained their bodies to run faster, go farther, and be stronger. I started a practice all my own. After a 30-90 minute nap to fight the fatigue that seemed to constantly be with me as I matured, I would get up, sit at a desk, and study for the next three hours.

I discovered very quickly that the best way for me to remember information was if I read it aloud. Gabe's room had become empty after he left for college, so I often snuck in there to be alone. I would read my textbooks and study my notes aloud, rehearsing page after page. I always had the luxury of shutting the door at home, so nobody had to hear my voice droning on and on about American history, human biology, or Algebra II. It was an annoying habit, but I was convinced it was the secret of my success. I was also convinced that I needed to be successful.

Failing to be healed of cerebral palsy felt deeply shameful. I felt as if I wore this failure as plainly as my disability. I was very aware that I couldn't stop limping, but I hoped that if I worked hard enough, my success in school would cover the failure that I felt in my heart. Slowly, I began to weave this robe; every A felt like the threads were getting thicker, covering my pain. Every other grade felt as if the threads were being loosened, threatening to unravel and expose that I not only failed to master the finer points of trigonometry, but also that I had failed at life. The threads seemed to be coming together as I wrapped up my senior year, but I began to wonder about the future.

Dad, how am I going to be able to read aloud to myself when I get to college?" I stared up at him from the passenger seat of the car while we waited at a red light.

"I don't know," he said, shrugging his shoulders. "I guess you'll have to find a room in a library."

From that moment on, I began my search for a college with the best library. After four college visits, I found what I was looking for at St. Cloud State University in Minnesota. Built in 2000, the James W. Miller Learning Resources and Technology Center looked more like a law firm than a campus hangout. Beautiful wooden tables lined open foyer space that spanned three floors. A desk lamp sat at each table, complementing the natural light that already streamed in through the windows. Computer labs were available on each floor and a winding granite staircase connected each level. When I walked into the first floor of the Miller Center during my campus tour, I knew St. Cloud State had potential, and when I gazed up to the second floor, I was filled with hope that I had found a home.

"What are those?" I eagerly asked the tour guide, pointing to the rooms on the top floor.

He smiled, "Those are study rooms. They're private rooms you can check out when you need to do projects in groups." His eyes scanned the crowd, waiting to take another question, but I interjected with a follow up.

"Can I reserve one for myself?"

"I'm sure you can…" the guide started to get annoyed.

"Who do I talk to about that?" I pressed.

He started to roll his eyes. "You'd have to check with the circulation desk." The guide looked exasperated, but I smiled in victory! My search for solitude was complete. And so, for hour after hour, day after day, I sat alone, locked away in a second-floor room, studying. Soon, the students at the circulation desk began to learn my name and eventually handed me keys without either one of us having to say a word. These study rooms became a sanctuary for me, a place all my own where I could make as much noise as I needed: rehearsing my notes to a silent audience, illustrating concepts on the board to an empty class, and verbalizing my thoughts to a vacant room.

When I wasn't studying, I was at church. I vowed to myself to never again attend a "Pentecostal" church, so that I would never have to worry about someone praying for my healing. I loved God, but healing continued to be the one subject I couldn't talk about with Him. So, I was delighted when a classmate invited me to a small evangelical church that was within walking distance from my dorm.

"God has a purpose and plan for your life!" the pastor preached with conviction from the stage. As I sat on the wooden pew listening, I was filled with courage. I didn't know what the years ahead had in store for me, but more than anything I wanted to believe that God was in control, despite what had happened between us. I hoped He could still use the part of me that wasn't damaged, the part that still liked to attend Sunday school, pray for guidance, and sing my heart out during worship. After just a few weeks, I knew it would be safe for me to attend this church without being hurt. No one was put on display week after week or blamed for their sicknesses. This church soon became my home and the people there "adopted" me like I was a kid belonging to a large family. I felt loved, sheltered, and hidden from my past because no one ever asked me about cerebral palsy, no one brought up the topic of healing, and most importantly, no one ever made me feel like a failure. All they saw was an eager college student and I was more than happy to keep it that way.

I sailed through my first semester of college with a 4.0. It seemed to me that college was easier than high school because all those hours studying back home were paying off. I headed home for Christmas thinking second semester would be a breeze.

It would have been if it wasn't for Dr. Micah.

Dr. Micah was a Jewish man, originally from Boston, who was filling in for the year while another professor was out on sabbatical. Several of the girls in the dorm recommended that I take his *History of Race in America* course. "It's easy!" "He's great!" "You'll love him!"

Liars.

My first clue that something was wrong should have been when I was asked to purchase and read 12 novels for his class, one of them being a very long book entitled *Malcolm X* by Alex Haley. *I'm a reader*, I shrugged. *No problem*.

Dr. Micah explained on the first day of class that we didn't have to take any tests and were only asked to write four short papers, one page each. *I got this one in the bag! I can write*. Then, just after the drop-date had passed when students could no longer change their schedules, Dr. Micah disclosed how he graded his students.

"I grade on a curve," Dr. Micah explained as he drew a slope across the chalkboard. "Only one of you will get an A, two of you will get an A-, most of you will get Bs and Cs," he paused at this point to turn to the class and smile, "but I'm not as cruel as other people, no one is going to fail; the lowest grade I'll give is a C-. When you write a paper for me, I will line them all up on a table and compare your work. The best one will receive an A, the worst one a C-, the rest of you will fall someplace in between."

The room fell silent. I sat in my chair, horrified, blinking over and over again at the diagram on the board, not quite believing what this man was saying. I wanted to bolt out the door and never come back. I gripped the sides of my desk, swallowing hard, willing myself to remain seated as I watched my knuckles turn white. I imagined Dr. Micah sitting at home, judging our work, paper by paper as they cluttered his dining room table in a massive line-up, making adjustments as he considered our writing. I sat there hoping my papers would somehow land on top, knowing my chances of this happening four times in one semester were slim, if not impossible. I was doomed. I might be a good writer, but was I the best? From where I sat, I figured I had two options: fight for an A in this course with everything I had or fail miserably as a human being.

I hated the idea that I had to somehow compete against my classmates to earn an A. Couldn't we all get the same grades? Usually, I enjoyed making friends with my classmates, but it was quickly becoming apparent that if I was going to succeed, I was going to have to view the people sitting next to me as my enemies: contending with them for Dr. Micah's attention, sparring with them to write the best papers, crushing any chances they had of winning. If Dr. Micah was only going to award one A in his class, then it was going to belong to me because I was going to capture it. It didn't matter what it took or who it hurt because there was a difference between me and everyone else in the room. My classmates may have wanted an A, but if I was going to keep my robe of perfection tightly woven, then I needed it.

For the rest of the semester, my heart never stopped pounding. Every Tuesday and Thursday I rushed through my meals at Garvey Commons, trying to consume as many calories as possible before my appetite began to wane as the clock ticked closer to 12:30. Usually, half of my food would hit the trash as I headed out the door across campus. As I opened the door to Stewart Hall, I could feel my chest tighten, and as I ascended the stairway to Dr. Micah's class, my knees would become weak. *Keep going*, I commanded myself. I gripped the wooden railing tighter as I forced myself to climb to the second floor.

Students were crowded around his door, anticipating his arrival. Waiting for him to appear was like waiting for punishment. As he came around the corner to unlock the classroom, I ordered myself to remain composed. *Keep your food in your stomach*, I yelled at myself silently as I waited to go in and sit down. The first five minutes of class always contained a quiz on the reading material from the previous day. I always found these questions easy. They were mainly asked as a motivator to get students to arrive on time and complete their homework. After the quiz, we usually sat in a circle and discussed the racial themes related to the novel we were reading. I eagerly shared my ideas and scribbled notes like a woman on fire while others were speaking, frantically gathering information for my next paper. One day, as the class hour came to an end, Dr. Micah concluded our discussion and then said, "Your next paper needs to answer the question: 'Why is Malcolm X considered an American hero?'"

As Dr. Micah revealed our next topic, I sat in my seat, once again feeling terrified, almost like I had when he announced that he graded on a curve. *I don't know the answer to this question,* I panicked. *Malcolm X called the white man a "devil." He later recanted his statement, but I have no idea why his image appears on a postage stamp and no idea how to write this paper, much less the best one in class.* I could feel my heart pounding inside my chest. My face felt flushed and I started to sweat. I saw Dr. Micah standing in the front of the class, giving a few more announcements, but I couldn't hear them because I was consumed with worry. As soon as the clock struck two, I hurried to the door and down the stairs to the library because my mind was screaming and I needed silence in order to think.

Why is he a hero? Why is Malcolm X an American hero!? I panicked, trying not to hyperventilate as I quickly typed words to my paper on my laptop. *Think Jenny, think! There has to be an answer.* I slowly relaxed as I made a list of possible suggestions in my notebook. I frantically searched the pages of Malcolm X in order to find evidence to support my ideas. *The Autobiography of Malcolm X was journey of transformation. Growing up, he struggled with the pain of racism in America. It wasn't until he took a pilgrimage to Mecca and witnessed people from all races worshiping together that he began to realize peace was possible. This changed his life and the way he interacted with others.* He had written, "I'm for justice, no matter who it is for or against. I'm a human being first and foremost, and as such I'm for whoever and whatever benefits humanity *as a whole.*"

The hours flew by; I had to renew my study room so I could finish my essay. By 5:00 PM, I had written a page on "Malcolm X the American Hero." I printed it out and dashed back across campus to Stewart Hall, hoping to catch Dr. Micah before he left for the day.

I tapped quietly on his office door. Dr. Micah looked up from his computer and nodded for me to come in. Trembling, I took a seat opposite of him.

"I was wondering if you could read my paper before I turn it in."

"Sure, I'll take a look at it."

I handed him my paper, watching his facial expressions as he scanned my words. My heart sunk as I watch him shake his head in disappointment.

"No. I'm sorry. You wrote this paper like you were still living in the 1960s. I want to know why Malcolm X is a hero today," Dr. Micah said as he returned my paper.

My mind began to spin. *I still don't understand why Malcolm X is a hero!* I started to ask Dr. Micah questions, grappling to salvage my work, hoping he'd change his opinion of my work. I didn't even finish before he cut me off, tired of listening to me speak.

"No, Jenny. This paper is not like your other papers. It's not any good.

You're not going to get an A this time." He nodded towards the door, "Get out of my office."

I rose from my chair, defeated at my abrupt dismissal. There was nothing I could do. I tried anxiously to revise my paper once I reached my dorm, but eventually I gave up and tried unsuccessfully to go to sleep. Around midnight, overwhelmed with stress and despair, I knelt down over a toilet and threw up.

My stomach clutched together like a belt twisted tightly around my waist. I could feel the acid rising through my esophagus as chunks of chicken patty and ice cream floated in the water below. *It's all over.* More food surged through my body as it landed in the bowl, adding to the colors in their frothy mix. *Everything I've worked for is falling apart*, I moaned. *My kingdom is crumbling.* My stomach squeezed again, almost choking me, but all I could offer was bitter spit. I dry heaved again and again, each time wishing I was someone else, crawling to get out of my own skin, desperate to escape my problems. When I finally felt empty, I wiped my face with a towel, rinsed out my mouth, and headed back to bed. I couldn't sleep. I could only lie on my bed, consumed with worry, waiting for morning to come and my next class to start.

I could hardly keep my eyes open during my 9:00 AM class. Dr. Vladimir was lecturing with his eyes closed about the unique animals that populate Australia. I listened with only part of myself. It was hard to concentrate on his voice because my own was crowding my mind. *Even if I'm a failure, I have to keep going. My dad is paying for this class, so I can't quit. I have to find a way to finish Dr. Micah's class.* I stared down at my backpack, thinking of ideas. *Maybe I can still earn an A in his class even though I won't get an A on this paper. Maybe if I work hard enough, put in more time, more energy, maybe there's still a way that I can succeed. Maybe my kingdom doesn't have to fall apart; maybe I can find a way to cope.*

For the rest of the semester, I lived in fear that I might not earn 4.0. Without a perfect grade point average, my robe would unravel leaving me shamefully naked for the world to see. This devastated me to the point of despair, but every morning, but I pressed on. When the alarm rang at 6:00 AM, I immediately got out of bed, feeling the familiar sorrow and anxiety beating inside my chest. My pulse quickened very early each day, even before I dressed to go outside. I pulled on my wind pants, threw on a sweatshirt, laced up my tennis shoes, and headed out the door into the snow. If I couldn't relax until the semester was over, at least I could physically exhaust my body throughout the day so that I could sleep at night.

I walked the steps to the gym, chilled by my stroll across campus. Wiping my shoes on the rug, I chose a treadmill and start to run. Normally I hated exercise,

I absolutely despised running, but I was convinced that I would lose my mind if I didn't move my body as hard as I could. *Slap, slap, slap,* I could feel my feet hit the rubber mat, jarring my ankle, but I didn't care. My muscles felt tight, having been at rest for eight hours, but I pushed them anyway. Slowly, my legs warmed and my speed increased. I pumped my arms, felt my face get hot, and my mind start to ease. For a brief moment, I experienced relief. The moment faded quickly because my body could not continue to run. Although my muscles were warm, my legs started to tighten, as if someone was slowly applying the brakes. I stepped off the treadmill, found a mat in the corner and began to stretch my legs and back. Then I headed out the door and across campus to Garvey Commons. There in the privacy of the cafeteria bathroom, I knelt on the floor, crying over the seat of the toilet, grieving the loss of my perfection, wishing I could throw up like I did that night in the dorms, but nothing ever came up from my stomach in the morning. When I was done sniffling, I headed out of the bathroom door and into the cafeteria to eat breakfast. This was my morning routine for several weeks. One day, I couldn't hide it any more.

"I...want...to...quit...college!" I sobbed to my parents while at home visiting for the weekend. My mom ran to grab the Kleenex from the window ledge while my dad stood in front of me, shaking his head.

"You're going to have to quit crying before we can talk."

"I can't stop," I wailed. "I need to cry." I wrapped my arms around my mom, hoping she would be more sympathetic.

"It's okay that you're crying," my dad said, "but I can't understand a word you're saying, so when you're done, we'll talk."

"Ok." I sat at the kitchen table for several minutes, sniffling, trying to compose myself.

"I don't understand," my dad said, taking a seat next to me. "What happened? Last semester you got a 4.0," he shook his head, "You said you *loved* college."

"I know," I said, looking down at the table. I didn't want to look at him again until I was ready. "It's different now. I don't think I can get an A in this class."

The room was silent for a moment.

"Jenny, we're still going to love you no matter what happens."

I nodded.

"We're still going to welcome you in, feed you, and take care of you."

"Ok." I said, knowing this was true, but still feeling miserable about myself.

"Jenny, maybe getting a B would be the best thing that could happen to you. You'd realize that it was not the end of the world," he paused, "You're not going to die if you don't have a 4.0."

"I can't sleep, I haven't been eating well."

He nodded, "That needs to stop. I think you just need to hand in your final paper and forget about what your final grade is going to be. All we ask is that you do your best."

"I know." Even though I was still consumed with anxiety, I knew I could finish the semester with my parents cheering me on. I walked over to my dad. He stood up and held me.

"You're going to be okay. We love you, no matter what."

As soon as my parents dropped me off at school at the end of the weekend, I began working on my final paper. My assignment was to answer the question, *"What does it mean to be American?"* I poured over my texts, trying to come up with an original answer. What could I learn from the story told in *Our America* about the boys who grew up in the projects of inner-city Chicago? Or from the Delany sisters, two African American women who came of age during the Depression? What conclusions could be drawn about the endless list of patents owned by African Americans, including the heart transplant and the salon sink? I asked people in the library for their opinions, scoured the Internet, and reviewed my notes. When I finally had enough information, I typed out my three-page, single-spaced paper, wrote my name across the top with a black Sharpie marker, and headed to class.

"Where's a good place to go out tonight?" Dr. Micah surveyed the class in place of his normal lecture.

"The Press!"

"The Carpet!"

What's going on? I sat in my chair, looking up with disappointment and confusion at the man I had held in high regard and fearful respect for the whole semester.

"Ok, what about afterwards? Does anyone have a place where I can crash on their floor for the evening?"

"You can stay at our place."

"Sure, come to our apartment!"

What's going on? I thought again.

A girl next to me raised her hand. "Are you coming back next year, Dr. Micah?"

"As a matter of fact, Tiffany, I'm not. But that has nothing to do with it. The semester is ending and I'm going to celebrate. I'm going to get drunk tonight somewhere between throwing up and passing out."

I sat in the front row, my mouth dropping open in disbelief. *I'm not even old enough to go to a bar; what is he doing recruiting us to come with him? I want out of here so bad.*

As soon as the class ended, I walked up to him and handed my paper. "Here you go, Dr. Micah; here's my final paper."

"Ok," he answered in surprise. There would be no feedback, no revision, no time spent talking to him during his office hours. I had been through enough and it was time to hand in my work. Whatever grade he gave me, I would accept. I had done my best, whether he agreed with me or not. I didn't know what to think about him after today's "lecture," except that I never wanted to see him again.

"Something came for you today from St. Cloud State," my mom said casually, handing me an envelope. I had come home for the summer to live with my parents and work at a local retail store. I looked down at the white envelope in my hands. The words *Office of Records and Registration* were scrolled across the return address line in red type. I held my breath. My heart pounded. I tore open the envelope, knowing my grades were inside. I unfolded the paper and as I read the print-out, I let out all the air I was holding. *He gave me an A! Dr. Micah gave me an A! I got a 4.0!*

I ran downstairs to my dad's office to check my e-mail. I wanted to tell my roommate that I had survived Dr. Micah's class! I logged into my account and there was a message from Dr. Micah himself:

Dear Jenny,

I want you to know that many students feel like they receive mixed messages from me. I'm hard on them when I grade their papers, yet tell them that I want them to do well in my course. Both are true. I held you to a higher standard than the other students in my class because I found that you needed the challenge. You are the best student that I ever had. If you should decide to be a teacher someday I believe you will be a good one! It is obvious to me that someone has taught you how to write!

Best,

Dr. Micah

I turned off the computer and breathed a sigh of relief. My academic success was still clothing me flawlessly and if I could survive this semester without it unraveling, then I was confident that I could handle any professor that came my way.

Chapter 9

"Hey, don't I know you from freshman year?" I looked at the stocky brunette woman sitting with her friends in Garvey Commons. The cafeteria was filling and I was looking for a place to sit.

"Yes," she nodded, smiling with recognition. "We had English together last year on Thursday nights. Have a seat," she gestured to the open spot at her table. "This is my friend Andy." I looked at Andy. I had seen him around campus, but we had never spoken. He walked with crutches; I was sure he had cerebral palsy. He also had an unforgettable shirt on that day—green with white lettering that read, "Gay? Fine with me!" *Interesting*, I thought. I knew nothing of the gay, lesbian, bi-sexual, transgender (GLBT) community on campus except that they represented themselves with rainbows and pink triangles on their doors, which meant you were entering into a "safe space" where all sexual orientations were tolerated. I had never met a man who was gay before and this intrigued me about Andy. But what piqued my curiosity even more was his gait. I had never really interacted with someone who shared my disability and I was eager to gain his perspective. *Was he a Christian? Had he ever asked God to heal him? Did he accept who he was and how he moved, or was he trying to hide it, like me?*

"Hi!" I said, sitting down. "My name's Jenny Hill. Nice to meet you, Andy." I extended my hand and he shook it. "What's your major?" This seemed like a safe way to begin the conversation.

"English education." He took a sip of his pop and then set it back on his tray. "Yours?"

"Information media. I want to be a school library media specialist."

Andy paused, trying to understand what I had just said. "A school librarian?"

"Yeah," I smiled. "You got it!"

"How did you decide you wanted to do that?"

I rolled my eyes, smiling. I got this question all the time and was starting to get sick of answering it. "With a lot of thought." I took a bite from my tray before continuing. "My parents are teachers."

"My mom works in the schools too."

I nodded. "I watched them growing up and really liked their lifestyle: family friendly, summers off, great work environment…but they told me not to go into elementary education because there are too many people with that degree."

"Yup."

"So, I thought about what I liked and decided that being a school library media specialist would be the perfect fit."

"Cool." Andy took a bit of his chicken patty sandwich before continuing. "Do you live on campus?"

"Yes. I live across the street in Mitchell Hall. How about you?"

"I live in Lawrence Hall. They just remodeled it; it's great!" Andy continued to chew his lunch. "Did you go to the residence hall dance last winter? I wonder if I saw you there?" Andy turned his head, trying to remember.

I didn't remember seeing Andy there, but I remembered the dance like it took place last weekend. "Yes. I was in pain that night."

"Why's that?"

"Do you remember how the weekend before it had stormed really bad?"

"Oh yeah!" he said, recalling. "There was ice everywhere!"

"I didn't see the ice on the steps outside of Garvey Commons on my way back to Mitchell Hall. I fell hard and hurt myself. I was in pain for weeks." I paused for a second, then continued. "Do you fall very often?"

"Yes, but that's why I got a handicapped parking permit. You should get one."

I stared at him, not believing what I'd just heard. *Me? Get a handicapped parking permit!? No way; I might have CP, but there is no way I am going to put it on display. I don't care if I have to trip and fall every week; I'd rather be injured than get a permit.*

"Why would I need one of those?" I asked, demanding an answer.

"Well," Andy answered. I could tell he was taken aback by my response, like I thought I was better than him. "For one thing, you would never have to pay for parking again."

I hadn't thought of that.

"I don't think you would fall as much either."

Ok. You've got me. My back has never been the same since.

"I mean, it's up to you." Andy shrugged his shoulders, "But I think you might like it."

"I'll think about it. Nice to meet you, Andy," I said as I got up from the table.

"Nice to meet you too."

I walked back to my dorm stunned. *I can't believe Andy is okay with having a handicapped parking permit. He seems to have totally accepted the fact that he has CP.*

He's not trying to hide it at all. I wonder what that's like?

"Why are you so dressed up?" My roommate Hannah was surprised to see me wearing dress clothes at 4:00 PM the following afternoon.

"I'm going to a scholarship dinner."

"For what?" she asked while picking up the TV remote.

"I got a scholarship from a local non-profit organization." I was careful not to mention *which* organization. I had gotten a scholarship for the second year in a row from United Cerebral Palsy of Central MN (UCP). It was also the second year in a row that I felt shame that I was receiving money because of my disability.

"They asked me to come to their dinner and share about how I'm doing in college," I continued. "It's at the Holiday Inn." *Maybe if I give enough details, Hannah won't ask any more questions.* I could feel my muscles tightening.

"Ok. Cool," she said, flipping the channels.

"I'll see you later tonight." I closed our dorm room door and walked down the stairs of Mitchell Hall into the lobby, waiting for my ride to pull up. Soon I saw a green Buick pull in front of the building. The passenger side window rolled down.

"Are you Jenny?" a middle-aged woman called out.

"Yup!"

"I'm Julia; hop in!"

I opened the car down and sat down. As soon as I got my seat belt buckled, Julia launched into conversation. Leaning over to me, she asked, "So, how did you get involved with UCP?"

I sat there for a moment, unable to answer because of my surprise. *What's going on? Doesn't she know I'm a scholarship recipient? Why else would she be picking me up from a college dorm?* Then, my stomach began to churn. My chest filled with a familiar low-level ache. I was going to have to do it. I was going to have to say the words I hated. The words that announced that I was a failure.

"I have cerebral palsy." *Oh,* I winced internally. *Those words hurt.* "I'm a scholarship recipient." The car was quiet for a moment. Neither one of us spoke.

"Oh," she answered, slightly embarrassed, "I wouldn't have noticed—you move so well."

Is that supposed to be some kind of a compliment?

"My son has cerebral palsy too."

"Is he in college right now?"

"No, he tried it for a semester but never finished." She looked over at me,

"Right now he's living in a friend's basement."

I nodded.

"I wish he'd continue. I wish he'd meet someone like you."

We rode in silence the rest of the way to the hotel. I distracted myself by looking out the window. I wasn't sure what to say to Julia. Talk about cerebral palsy? I'd rather write another paper for Dr. Micah. Talk about her son? It sounded like she was trying to set us up. I was happy to discover that when we arrived, we were assigned spots at different tables. Sitting next to me was an elderly lady easily in her eighties. She wore a button-down blouse, cotton skirt, and orthotic shoes. Her hair was curly white and her hands were speckled with age spots. Her place setting read: *Dottie Wren, Former Physical Therapist.*

"Hi, it's nice to meet you, Dottie." I held out my hand to shake, beaming with a smile. Dottie recoiled at the sound of my greeting, looking over me from head to toe as if she were appraising a used car.

"Why are *you* here?" she demanded.

Answer her quickly, or she's going to get mad! "I have CP," I rushed. The words felt so much easier when I only had to use the abbreviation. "I'm a scholarship recipient."

"You *do?*" she snapped, waiting once more for my response.

"Yes," I said uneasily. *Maybe I should be ashamed. Maybe this money should go to someone else.*

"Well, you must not have it very bad then, do you?" She concluded with sass.

I sat at the table with my mouth hanging open. I had no idea what to say. Luckily, Dottie saved me from my predicament as she turned her back to me and talked with the person on the other side of her for the remainder of the night. I sat there thinking about the strange world I lived in while eating my baked chicken and green beans. I had spent the majority of my childhood praying that God would somehow rid me of my cerebral palsy, desperately trying to fit in with the "normal people," but always feeling like I stuck out. Tonight, it seemed like the proverbial shoe was on the other foot. Tonight I didn't stick out *enough.* But here was the catch: I didn't fit in with this group either. I didn't fit in anywhere.

I looked around the room as cake was served and coffee was poured. I saw parents sitting at tables with their children pulled up next to them in motorized wheelchairs needing to be fed. I watched the gait of the people who came and went from the bathroom. Many of them had the trademark tangled movement that accompanied cerebral palsy. It was easy to distinguish because every case was so much more severe than my own. I looked to my right and saw a smiling man in his wheelchair. He was pressing buttons on a board in front of him, which in turn "spoke" with a synthesized voice. The shame and confusion that I held in my head and my heart was starting to melt and transform into something else. A different overwhelming sensation was tugging at my chest. This time, it wasn't the pain of failure. It was the conviction of humility. Questions that I had repeated over and over in my mind for years were starting to rearrange into different patterns. *"Why can't I walk like everyone else?"* transformed to *"Why do I walk so well?"*

For my whole life it had seemed that I was doomed to struggle every time I moved, forced to watch those around me enjoy living in their bodies. I had always wondered why God hadn't made me like everyone else. Tonight, as I looked around the room, I was still wondering "Why me?" but it was from a whole new perspective. *Why am I not in a wheelchair? Why do I have the privilege of enjoying public speaking while others can't speak at all? Why do I fret so much about how I move? Half the people in this room would kill to walk like I do.* I had always thought I was losing at the game of life because I had CP, that the odds were never in my favor. Tonight, I sat in awe of the great hand I had been dealt. Why God had chosen to spare me from the full severity of CP, I could not understand, but I was overwhelmingly grateful for all the ability He had given me.

"Jenny," I startled as I felt a hand on my shoulder, "there's someone here that I think you should meet." I turned around to see Julia standing next to a young couple. "This is Peter and Anita Baxter. Peter's parents are professors at St. Cloud State."

"Oh yes!" I looked up smiling, "The Baxters. Sure. Your mom taught one of my classes last summer. Nice to meet you." I got out of my chair, turning to face them so we could talk. I figured it was okay to lead off with the inevitable, "So, how are you connected to UCP?"

"Well, we have two beautiful twin daughters, Alexa and Rachel." Anita pulled a picture from her wallet; two girls with golden blonde curls were staring back at me, smiling. "Rachel was born without any complications," Anita pointed her out in the picture, "but Alexa had a stroke in utero." I nodded with concern. "She has a condition similar to cerebral palsy where her muscles tighten and spasm."

I listened but was a little confused. Anita must have recognized the look on my face because she continued to explain.

"At first, the doctors thought she had cerebral palsy, but then her symptoms started to progress."

"Oh," I said, starting to understand. CP was a stagnant condition. If things started to change, there had to be something else wrong.

"The doctors think that she has something called dystonia."

"Hmm," I said, turning my head and thinking, "I've never heard of that before."

"We hadn't either," Peter added.

We were silent for a moment and then I burst into chatter, unsure what to say. I knew personally what it was like to have a disability, but I had no idea what it was like for a parent to watch helplessly as their daughter struggled with her body.

"Someone told me tonight that I move *well*," I began to gesture animatedly with my hands. "I never know how to answer that. What exactly does that mean?" I leaned in, trying to gain their insight, "That I'm the 'Queen of the Klutz Club?' What am I supposed to say, 'Thank you!?'"

Anita rolled her eyes with an understanding smile. "Yeah, I don't always know what to say either."

"Good to know I'm not the only one." I smiled, relieved that I had found a friend. "So how old are your girls?"

"They're four years old," Peter said.

Wow! Four years old! I remember that—it was filled with doctors and hospital visits and a cast. "When I was four, I had an orthopedic operation to improve my gait. My surgeon broke my femurs, rotated my hips out, and lengthened my tendons so my feet could stand flat on the floor." I paused for a second, watching Peter's face. It was filled with a pain that I couldn't understand. Concern, I guessed, for the road ahead for Alexa. I slowed down, containing my emotion.

"I was put in a body cast for six weeks to heal and then had physical therapy after that." I turned, looking into their eyes, wanting to offer something hopeful. "I suppose it was overwhelming at the time, but it was worth it. I'd do it again; I really mean that. It changed my life." I stared down at my legs. "I went from walking like a 'freak of nature' to where I am today. It's great!"

Peter and Anita nodded reassuringly, inviting me to say more. I continued, "When I started elementary school, I remember my parents telling me that if anyone ever made fun of the way I walked, I needed to remember that they were the ones that had the problem. I think they wanted to make sure that I never viewed my life through the lens of my limitations." I looked forward to see pairs of eyes, nodding in agreement.

"I think it was helpful," I shrugged, "I'm in college now; I'm independent, so it all worked out."

"My mom talks about you all the time," Peter said.

"You should come over some time and meet the girls," Anita chimed in. "They need to meet a role model like you."

"I'd like that very much. Nice to meet you."

"Nice to meet you too, Jenny."

We parted ways and I returned to my dessert. *I'm such a phony. I'm no role model. I may look successful sitting here with my straight As and my little scholarship.* I took one final bite of my cheesecake before setting down my fork. *Rachel and Alexa don't want to be like me at all. I hate myself.*

Chapter 10

SPED 201: Special Education for the Secondary Teacher. I looked down at the words scrolled across the top of the canary yellow syllabus on the table in front of me. Like it or not, everyone pursuing a teaching license of any kind was required to take one special education course. *Here comes the speech.* I could almost give it myself, now that I was a college senior, no need to hear it from a professor. *This course is the* most important one *that you will take before you graduate.* It was the same message I had heard from the professor who taught Health for Teachers and identical to the one given by my English Language Learners prof. I got it. Everyone was passionate about their subject area. Every class was the most important one. Yada yada yada.

"Good evening, class." I looked up from the syllabus to see a professor standing in the front of the room. "My name is Beth Carlson and this is SPED 201. I'm very glad you're here," Beth spoke smoothly and deliberately, often using her hands. "I know you've taken many courses in order to pursue your licensure." *Here we go again.* I began to roll my eyes. "But this course is one that I feel will be the most important one that you take before you graduate." *How original.*

Beth began to pace the room, moving from side to side, making an effort to make eye contact with everyone. "This course really has two components. One is the course work and class time involved. You'll be expected to read your entire textbook and attend all lectures," she paused. "This course is designed to give you a broad overview of all the disabilities you may encounter while working in the public school setting."

"If you turn to page two of your syllabus," suddenly a ruffling of canary yellow papers was heard throughout the room, "you will find the requirements for the other component of this course." The room was quiet for a moment while everyone read the information in front of them. "As you can read in the syllabus, you're required to complete a field experience while in this course, spending at least 20 hours outside of class with people who have disabilities."

"Really!?" I whispered with frustration to the person sitting next to me.

"I know, right?"

"I don't have time to do this; they should post this in the course description before we register."

Beth Carlson continued speaking, "It doesn't have to be in a school setting, you could volunteer with Special Olympics or with a non-profit organization; it's up to you."

Audible groans could be heard throughout the classroom. No one seemed too interested in the assignment. Including myself.

"Now I'm sure that you all have had experiences interacting with people who have disabilities. To start off tonight, I want you to turn to the person sitting next to you and share about someone you know who is disabled."

I turned to my table partner and began to listen. He told about his uncle who had slight hearing loss. When he was done, it was my turn. I told him that I had mild CP and how I was pulled out during the school day to work with the adaptive physical education teacher in order to stretch my legs. I told him about having an individualized education plan where my locker was in a centralized location so I didn't have to walk too far to get to class. It seemed okay talking to one person privately about my limitations, so I decided to continue talking, opening up a bit more. "There are some quirky things about living with CP that I don't fully understand," I said with a smile.

"Like what?"

"Like I can't seem to remember what corner of an envelope a stamp is supposed to go on."

"Weird!"

"I know! I have to look at old pieces of mail to figure it out every time." I rolled my eyes, laughing. "I also jump really easy. People seem to have a lot of fun with this, and I didn't realize it was connected to anything related to CP until I was learning to drive."

My table partner turned his head with curiosity.

I turned towards him, becoming more animated. "Well, everyone is usually so excited about getting their driver's license, right?"

He nodded.

"Not me." I paused. "I know many of my friends were 'chomping at the bit' to get their license, scheduling their road test on their birthday, but if it were up to me," I paused for a moment, "I wouldn't have ever gotten my license."

"Why?"

I nodded. "It's confusing to me too, but my reaction time is a bit slower than yours and when I'm driving through busy or unfamiliar places, I get nervous."

"That makes sense."

"My muscles tense up when I'm nervous and then I don't feel safe driving sometimes. I want to be independent, but I don't want to be dead, right?"

"Right."

"Eventually I did learn to drive, but once," I paused to chuckle, "a cop thought I was a drunk driver!"

"No way!" His eyes got big as he slammed his hands down on the table.

"Yes!" I leaned forward, excited to tell a good story. "I was driving home at night on this country road, *with my mother*, and I couldn't see the road very well because it was dark."

"Go on."

"To top it off, I was driving the family van and I wasn't really sure how much pressure to use on the gas pedal. Eventually I saw these lights flashing," I shrugged, "I figured, they're not for me. I'm not doing anything wrong."

His eyes grew bigger as I kept talking.

"Eventually my mom sees what's going on and she says, 'Jenny, pull over!' and I'm like, 'What!?' I'm getting pulled over!? What for!?' Turns out the cop thought I was drunk."

"That's a great story!"

"Yeah," I smiled, "eventually I went to the Courage Center and had a driving evaluation to make sure that I *should* be driving and that's where I found out that my jumping had to do with CP."

"What happened?"

"Well, I sat down in this private room with an occupational therapist and she starts asking me all of these questions. Most of them were routine: What's your diagnosis, are you taking any medication and so on, then all of the sudden she asks, 'Do you startle easy?' I just stopped.

How could she know to ask me that? It turns out I have something called a 'startle reflex' and it's really common! Who knew?"

"Who knew." He shook his head and smiled. It looked like class was about to resume. Conversations were wrapping up around the room and Beth Carlson had returned to the front.

"I think you've had enough time to share your ideas. Now I am going to call on some of you to share with the whole class what you have just shared with your partner."

I sat in my chair and froze. *Don't call on me, don't call on me*, I silently prayed. Beth must have noticed that I was concentrating hard because I was the first name called.

"You in the back." I saw her finger unmistakably pointing at me. "Who did you share about with your partner?" I held my breath. There was no way of getting out of this one. My chest began to fill with the familiar pain of shame that

I had felt in the car when I had to explain to Julia Fields from UCP that I wasn't just some volunteer who cared about people with disabilities. I was someone with disability.

"I shared about myself," I began slowly. Beth's face changed as she realized the sensitivity of her question. *You weren't expecting that one, were you?* I thought. "I have mild cerebral palsy." Pain grabbed at my chest as the words spilled out of my mouth like a quiet confession. *God, that hurts to say.*

"It mainly affects my hand-eye coordination and my reaction time." I noticed that the room had fallen silent. Every eye seemed to be staring back at me. "I shared about being on an independent education plan and working with the adaptive physical education instructor in order to stretch my muscles. Umm..." I paused, "I also talked about learning how to drive. It took me a little longer than most people because my reaction time is a little delayed, but I eventually got my driver's license."

Beth stared back at me, listening closely to what I was sharing. The moment was feeling increasingly awkward. "So I guess I didn't just share about someone I know, I shared about myself." With that, I nodded my head with finality and fell silent.

"Thank you for sharing, that was very brave of you. I think your experiences will add much to the classroom." Beth smiled at me and then selected another student to share.

"Andy, how can they expect us to just add a 20-hour field experience to the rest of our schedule!?"

"I know," Andy said, "I took that course last semester; it was kind of a drag."

It was Saturday evening and we were going through the dinner line at Garvey Commons. Andy and I had become close as our college careers had progressed and we often ate together in the cafeteria. We soon spotted a table and I continued to vent to Andy about how inconvenient this assignment was and how I thought it was unfair.

"Hey can we sit here?" My banter was interrupted by a trail of guys carrying dinner trays and wearing "Alphabet Soup" T-shirts. There was a GLBT conference going on that weekend on campus and these guys were clearly attendees. Red lanyards advertising "gay, lesbian, bi- sexual, transgendered, queer, and allied" were around their necks and rainbow key chains hug from the pockets of their jeans.

There were about five guys in the line-up. Most I had never met before, but one I clearly recognized. I didn't know his name, but we had definitely seen each other last year at a Campus Crusade for Christ event that he was leading. He looked up, saw me, and almost dropped his tray. I watched as his face turned pink, then red, then almost purple with embarrassment. His chest pumped in and out underneath his T-shirt as he struggled to catch a breath. He was clearly tortured at the thought of me associating him with a ministry and it was time to put him out of his misery.

"Have a seat," I almost demanded, pulling out a chair for him.

"Wh..what?" he stammered in disbelief.

"Have a seat," I repeated, extending my arm again to the chair sitting next to me. He obediently placed his tray on the table and sat down, still struggling to catch his breath. He sat there for a minute, just panting. I took a bite of the hot dish in front of me while I waited for him to speak.

"I, I didn't want you to see me like this. It's not what you think. I..."

"It doesn't matter what I think," I interrupted. "You are always welcome to sit at this table."

"Ok."

We ate for a few moments in silence. Andy was busy talking to some of the other guys who had also taken a seat at our table.

"I don't even think we've ever been formally introduced before. My name's Jenny Hill. I think we met at the CRU outreach event last spring. You were handing out Bibles."

"Jake Larson. Nice to meet you, Jenny." He extended his hand and I shook it. "I remember that night. I remember talking to you too. That's why I was so scared when I saw you at the table. I thought maybe you'd judge me."

"Well, like I said, you're always welcome to eat dinner with me." I took a sip of water. "So, what's your story, Jake? Have you told any of the adult leaders in CRU that you're gay?"

"Yeah. I've told one," he said quietly, looking down at the table.

"How'd that conversation go?" I asked gently.

"I told him that I was scared of being lonely."

I looked at Jake wide-eyed. This wasn't the answer I was expecting. "Why are you afraid that you're going to be lonely?"

"Look, I know homosexuality is a sin." Jake was staring straight into my eyes. "The person I told and I both agree that if I feel attracted to men, there's only one thing I can do—be alone. I can never have a partner, I can never have children, and I can never talk about it at work," he said with confidence. I sat there shocked.

"I want to be a teacher," he explained. "That's a very conservative profession. If people find out that I'm gay, they won't want their children in my class."

I began to nod, starting to understand what Jake was saying.

"I have to hide who I am. I hate it. I hate myself. I wish I wasn't like this. I wish I wasn't gay. There's nothing I can do about it."

I met Jake's comments again with silence. Andy was the first person I had ever met who was gay, and he seemed to be enjoying it. I had never asked Andy about his faith because our friendship seemed to be based on something else—our shared experiences of becoming teachers and the everyday hassles of living with CP. Jake was the first person I ever knew who articulated his internal struggles to me. He was the only person who had ever confessed his self-hatred to me—a feeling that I knew all too well. As for feeling the need to hide, I knew about that too. It seemed that I was spending every waking moment expending tremendous amounts of energy trying to hide behind my achievements. *If I work really hard at school, everyone will respect me. No one will think less of me because I have CP. I can cover my shame with a robe of perfection.* Sitting there next to him, I felt as if I hadn't just heard a guy confess his sins and insecurities; I had also heard my own.

"This classroom has 10 children in it. They're all high-functioning students with learning and other disabilities." I looked around the room, taking in the scene. To complete my assignment, I had chosen to come to a middle school special education classroom. I had spent the last 16 years of my life in public schools, but this was the first time I had ever seen the inside of a SPED room. I was used to seeing rows of desks, lined up and facing the chalkboard, but the layout of this room was different. Yes, there were desks in the room, but few of them. Tables lined the outside of the rows where students sat in small groups reading with a paraprofessional. *One, two, three, four adults,* I mentally counted. *Wow! The student-to-teacher ratio in this room is great!* I stepped inside the room and walked around, wanting to get a closer look. "The caaaattt ran out the door," one student sounded out.

"Good, Billy, go on," a teacher encouraged him.

I glanced at the material Billy was reading. Even though he was in middle school, his book resembled what I had seen first graders reading. The first words of sentences were bolded and underlined, helping students understand where sentences began and ended.

Walking further, I saw an old computer station towards the back of the room. A girl with Down Syndrome was playing an addition game. "Jill, it's time to get off the computer now," a voice called. Jill continued to play as if she had heard nothing. She continued to play for several minutes. "Jill, I said it was time to be done on the computer." This time the teacher's voice was more direct and demanding. She continued to play, ignoring her direction. *How long are you going to just let her sit there and play?*

I continued to circle the room and found two students playing with a large bin of rice. They took turns burying their fingers in the rice, then turning their palms over to let the grains sift through their hands and fall back into the tub. Occasionally they would take a cup, fill it with rice and let the grains fall out of the cup, watching as the grains hit the surface. "What are they doing?" I asked the teacher.

"They have autism. Patrick, the boy on your left," she said pointing, "is non-verbal." I stared at Patrick, wondering what it would be like if I couldn't speak. "Sometimes children with autism need a sensory break. They get over-stimulated. Playing with the rice helps them calm down."

I knelt down and picked up some grains of rice for myself, remembering what it was like to be a child. The rice had a definite texture to it and letting it run through my fingers reminded me of sand. "It's interesting," I said, looking at the teacher and smiling. "I can see why they like it."

She smiled back. "It's soothing, isn't it? Now," she turned and pointed her finger, changing the subject, "what I'd like you to do while you are here is help students one-on-one with their homework assignments."

"Sounds good. I can do that."

"Many of the students attend a general education class with a para and get extra help if they need it. They are still required to do the same homework as everyone else with some modifications," the teacher paused before continuing. "Right now the eighth graders are learning about sexuality and I think it's a little *too* much for some of our students, so I have some of them doing a worksheet identifying plants instead." *Alrighty. I'm glad she's not asking me to explain the birds and bees. Plants it is!*

"One of those students is this one right here." I was escorted over to a student desk a couple of feet away. "Miss Hill, I'd like you to meet Joshua." I extended my hand to greet him. "Joshua, this is Miss Hill. She's going to help out in our class for a few days."

"Ok," he said, wiggling his nose, looking at me with curiosity, wondering what I was really doing there. "I'm doing a worksheet on plants."

"Yeah, I understand that." I looked down at Joshua's worksheet. His handwriting was large and nearly illegible. Suddenly, I felt his index finger extend and poke me in my side. I jumped a mile. He had discovered one of my secrets. All I needed was the slightest poke in order to go flying.

Joshua watched my reaction with amusement. "Ha, ha, you're funny!" he said, pointing and laughing.

"I'm glad you think so," I smiled down at him, grateful we had made a connection. "Now, let's get to work."

So, for the next month, I visited Joshua, along with the other students in his classroom, for a few hours a day, twice a week. He'd usually greet me with a poke and I'd always jump, even though I knew it was coming. Sometimes, if I concentrated hard enough, I could control my body and remain still. When this happened, Joshua would get confused and would repeatedly jam his index finger into my side, trying to get a reaction. "You're not doing it!" he would complain between jabs. "How come you're not doing it?"

"I'm sorry," I would say, holding up my hands, shrugging, "I can't help it."

Most days, we spent the entire length of time in one classroom, completing worksheets or reading in groups. Since this particular school welcomed many students with varying levels of disabilities, there were times when we traveled down the hall to visit other classrooms. One day, while walking down the hall as a group, I felt another poke at my side. Feeling slightly different, I turned to see that the poker was not Joshua, it was another girl named Amanda.

Looking down at her, waiting to hear her speak, I watched as her mouth started to move. She was struggling to form words. "Why...do...you...walk...like... that?" I felt as if I had just heard the longest sentence in my life. It was hard for me at first to realize what she had just asked. Amanda's words felt like they came to me through a radio struggling to capture its signal.

I gulped. Amanda's question had caught me off-guard. *Well, if I can't tell her, who can I tell?* I ignored the familiar shameful pain rising in my chest, looked Amanda straight in the eyes, and went for it. "I have cerebral palsy, Amanda. I was born pre-mature. That's why I walk this way."

Amanda began to flap her arms excitedly. A big smile broke across her face and her eyes started to twinkle. "Me...too!" The words came out of her mouth in slow motion. Amanda ran off to tell her teacher, excited about the news.

I walked the rest of the way down the hall, uncertain how to handle what had just taken place. *I have never seen anyone so happy or encouraged by the fact that I have cerebral palsy. Should I continue to try to hide it? Should I continue be ashamed?* Like Jake had confessed in Garvey Commons, I often wished God had created me differently. I wished I didn't face the challenges of CP just like I was sure he must wake up every morning wishing he wasn't gay. But, what was I supposed to think when I met people like Amanda? Ignore her joy?

Chapter 11

"Jenny, do you know why you're here?" Beth Carlson sat across from me in her office, her hands pressed against each other in a tent of fingers. Last semester she had been my prof, but some staffing changes had occurred over Christmas break, and she was now serving as interim Dean for the College of Education.

"No. Your assistant just said that you wanted to meet with me."

Beth nodded. "Jenny, your professors and I would like to nominate you to speak at commencement."

I sat there in the chair, looking at Beth, a little shell-shocked. My eyes widened and my pulse quickened. *Wow! Could this really be happening? All my hard work has paid off at last!*

"Now, I realize that not everyone enjoys public speaking," Beth turned her head and looked at me, "and it's an honor just to be nominated. I asked you come to my office today to see if you are interested in continuing on in this process."

I swallowed, trying to keep my excitement contained. Of course I was interested! I thought of all the hours I had spent in the library studying, all the social opportunities I had declined, and the sacrifices I had made over the past four years to stay at the top. I had come to college with one goal in mind: to prove to myself and to the world that I wasn't a failure. Not only was I interested in being the commencement speaker, it was an honor I felt I had earned and deserved.

"Yes, I'm very interested!" I nodded, smiling.

"Good! Now, we need to get right to work. There's a bit of an audition process that you will need to go through. Every college at the university is allowed to nominate one student to give the commencement address." Beth paused to make sure that I understood this was going to be competitive. Well, if it was a fight she wanted, I was a contender!

"All the nominees are asked to propose what they will be speaking about in front of a panel. *Most* students just share a few words about what they might speak about. I want *you* to have your whole speech prepared so they can get a sense about how you address a crowd."

I nodded.

"Go home. Write a speech, and come back next week and we'll practice." For the next several days, I was glued to my laptop. When I went home over the weekend, I sat at the same desk where I pondered scripture as a child...*I have fought the good fight, I have finished the race, I have kept the faith....*

My fingers danced across the keys as I began to compose: "Good afternoon and congratulations on a job well done! I am proud to be a part of the graduating class of 2006!"

Yes, this was the finish line! As I sat at my desk at home, I thought about the many steps I had taken to get to this day: the countless room reservations I had made in the library, the hours I had spent alone just so I could understand a concept just a little bit more, becoming a little more ready for class the next day. I thought about the struggle I had during Dr. Micah's class, how he had encouraged me to write, challenging me to get better, and here I was four years later. I thought about how much energy I had expended and now it was over. I could never run this course again because the journey had taken all I had. And yet, the word commencement itself meant "beginning." Maybe the line I was about to cross was really the entrance to another race entirely? I thought again about Dr. Koop and the hours of training he had endured, how his example had continually pushed me forward, even when I felt like slowing down. Medical school was only the doorway to his career.

I also thought about how the robe I would be wearing in a few weeks was symbolic of how academics had covered my shame and helped me to look successful. Even if I had been motivated by my pain, wasn't all of this about something deeper, the chance to share what I had with others? Paul was one of the most educated people in the Bible and I imagined that if he were chosen to speak at a commencement ceremony in front of his peers, he would have to include his famous line, "Without love, I am nothing."

I continued to ponder this as I wrote, reading my words back to myself as I had done so many time before. Did my words make sense? Did they flow together? I looked up and saw a poster hanging on my wall near my desk. A rhythmic gymnast was prancing across the floor in a pink leotard. The poster read: Start with love; end in victory. Yes! I think I'll end on that note. *If we want to be successful in life, we have to love each other first.*

"You can come in now, Jenny."

"Thank you." I got up from my seat out in the hall and walked into the boardroom in the campus administration building. I looked around the table, taking in the array of professors and administrators that sat around a large wooden table. All of them were wearing business suits, looking a little bored as they swiveled in their leather chairs. *One, two, three, four, five*, I began to count familiar faces, hoping this would help my chances.

Beth and I had worked hard together in preparation for this day. I had spent hours in her office, and we would often travel to large classrooms within the education building so I could grow accustomed to speaking in generous spaces. She had coached me, encouraged me, and even invited colleagues to listen from time to time. Everyone had offered helpful feedback. Looking out at the faces, I could see Beth seated near the back. Her professional, neutral expression offered me little comfort.

I looked around the room once more, swallowed my nerves, and began to speak. I had rehearsed the words so often that they had become second-nature to me. I glanced down at my script from time to time, but made an effort to make eye contact with everyone in the room at least once. When I was done, I held my papers at my side and waited.

A polite golf clap arose from those seated at the table. No one smiled. Even though I felt confident in my delivery, I wasn't sure how to read their response.

"Thank you, Jenny. We'll let you know what we decide."

I walked out the door; all that was left to do now was to sit around and wait.

A few hours later, the black-corded phone on the desk where I worked on campus was lighting up. The caller ID displayed the words I had been waiting for all morning. *Dean's Office, College of Education*. Trembling, I picked up the receiver and placed it against my ear, trying to remain calm, or at least fake it.

"Hi, this is Jenny," I managed to croak out.

"Jenny, this is Beth." *Get to the point, yes or no already!*

"I have good news." I closed my eyes and breathed a sigh of relief. "They loved you! You're going to be the commencement speaker!"

"Yes!" I screamed into the phone, unable to contain my emotion any longer. The last week I had felt like I was in a pressure cooker and it was time to let out some steam. As soon as I was done screaming, I looked up, realizing what I had done—I had just screamed into the phone at the Dean of Students, and everyone within earshot, and perhaps beyond, had heard me. I looked to my left; student workers were staring at me, wondering what was going on.

Coming to my senses, I remembered this was a professional office and Beth was still on the phone, waiting to say more to me. "Sorry, Beth. I got a little excited."

"That's okay, Jenny," Beth said, chuckling. "I'm excited for you too. You'll be getting a letter in the mail later this week from the president confirming our decision. Congratulations."

"Thanks, Beth." I held the phone to my ear long after Beth hung up, frozen in my seat. I couldn't believe what had taken place this morning. In a month, I would speak in front of 7,000 people. The idea felt scary and vindicating all at once!

"Are you nervous?" another graduate asked, standing next to me on commencement day in cap and gown. We were all huddled in a back room of the hockey center, waiting to file into our seats.

"Nervous?! No!" I responded, almost offended at the question. "I worked so hard for this. I'm about to be honored in front of everybody; this is the best day of my life."

"Good," she said, giving me a hug. "I'm glad you're not nervous. You should enjoy this day." Soon "Pomp and Circumstance" could be heard blaring through the hockey arena's speakers.

I followed in step behind the first row of graduates. We looked like penguins in Harry Potter costumes as we marched into the stadium to take our seats. I took my place on the end of a row, sat down in my folding chair, and waited, looking up at the sea of people in the stands all around us. My parents had been given special seats in the players' box so they could easily see the stage. Everyone was talking in excited tones and texting their friends as masses of students found their seats. Twenty minutes later everyone was settled.

The university president walked to the podium and began to speak. "Ladies and gentlemen, good afternoon."

Responses of "Good afternoon" were heard en masse like an obedient echo.

"It's a time-honored tradition that we ask one of our own to students to address the crowd this afternoon. Jennifer Hill will graduate today with a Bachelor of Science degree in Information Media. Please welcome her to the stage."

At the sound of my name, I got up from my chair and proudly walked up the steps to the stage. I was beaming and I couldn't stop! *This is really happening! I really did it!* I walked up to the podium, set down my script, adjusted the mike, and looked out into the audience. An ocean of mortarboard-capped 20-somethings stared back at me. I was the center of attention and I relished it. Sure, I was confident many would text their way through my address, tapping their feet impatiently as they waited to get their diplomas. Some might stare at me, feigning interest as I spoke, and a few would honestly be listening.

Whatever their state of attention, I was going to savor this moment. I was the one who had worked hard; I was the one with the perfect GPA. It was my turn to stand on the stage and shine. This moment was so different from when I timidly walked on stage as a 12 year old, shamefully revealing my short-comings to a crowd. Today my shame was concealed under my robe, hidden behind a flawless academic career, and I was ready to confidently show a room full of people someone who hadn't failed. I shared my thoughts that had been carefully crafted and rehearsed time and time again in Beth's office and in front of the mirror. Point by point, I delivered my encouragements and then concluded:

> *How do we become successful business people, revolutionary scientists, inventive engineers, compassionate medical professionals, effective teachers, and creative artists? We become these things as we love those around us by placing their needs ahead of our own. We become successful when we share all that we have been given: the love from our family and friends, the knowledge we've gained from our college education, and the expertise we develop during our careers with those in our sphere of influence. If you start with love, I guarantee you will end in victory. Congratulations class of 2006; class is dismissed!*

Applause erupted from the audience. Cheering, I was certain, for the fact that I had *finished* speaking. I knew, however, in that moment, that I had completed more than just a speech. An entire chapter in my life had just ended. My days of studying for hours, needing to prove my self-worth by earning As, were done. I had become not only the best student I could be but also the best student possible. I had worth, I finally decided, because I had the transcript to prove it.

Chapter 12

$\mathcal{M}$y brother Gabe has quite a sense of humor. Once I graduated, he gave me a card that said, "It's hard to imagine that all your hard work has finally paid off...leaving you here." Inside was a picture of a cubical with a folding chair. *Oh man*, I moaned. I wondered what it would be like to spend your professional life in a human-sized cage. It didn't seem like the natural order of things. How could you ever feel like you had "arrived" professionally when you sat and stared all day at a cardboard wall, hearing everything everyone else was saying? How did anyone concentrate with all the distractions? Apart from the noise, I could just imagine my back getting stiff and my hamstrings tightening while sitting in a chair, eyes glued to the computer screen, hour after hour. Surely cubical dwellers were connected to an IV of pain meds just to get through the day.

When I started working as a graduate assistant three months later, I quickly learned there were no IVs in cubical land, just bottles of ibuprofen stashed away in desk drawers. St. Cloud State did not license undergrads to become school library media specialists, so while I had closed a successful chapter in my academic career, my journey wasn't over. I had two more years to finish my coursework and earn my master's degree. Many of my classmates couldn't wait to leave the university and start working, but I couldn't think of anything I wanted to do more than continue my education. I loved being a college student. Instead of rejection, I found acceptance. Instead of failure, I found success. College had become an incubator, and at 22, I wasn't ready to leave the womb.

Graduate school, I decided would be different. I aimed to do well but was not shooting for perfection. I already proved to myself that I was capable of straight As. Now I could exhale and relax, enjoying school without the pressure. During the day I worked in "cubical land" writing a departmental newsletter, answering e-mails, and completing clerical work. Often, it seemed, I was paid to study on the job. I loved what I was doing, rubbing shoulders with professors during the day while taking classes at night.

My life seemed pretty easy. Graduate school was seldom challenging. Library science was not rocket science and pursuing a master's degree was nothing like my undergraduate experience. The program was shorter, the classes were easier. Texts acted more as a reference and less as a book to be read from cover to cover. My classmates were working professionals and, best of all, Dr. Micah taught none of my classes. Gone were the days of auditorium-style learning and Scantron bubble sheets. Graduate school was about lectures, discussion, and writing. Could it get any better?

But unfortunately, if I learned nothing in graduate school, I did learn this: the old adage is true; when you're on top, you have a long way to drop. Just when my robe of academic perfection seemed the most secure, my personal life began to crumble.

"The love of my life is having an affair!"

I was jolted away from my computer screen on the Monday morning following Thanksgiving break. My fellow graduate assistant, Mary, leaned against the wooden door of the office and sobbed, her face transforming from its normal pale color to splotchy red. Her husband was working on his doctorate at a college on the East Coast. He had fallen in love with a student there.

I sat at my desk and listened to her story, watching her cry. What was I supposed to say? I may have been full of book smarts, but I was an idiot when it came to relationships. The only men I had ever been around were gay. I loved hanging around them when I needed a date, craved testosterone, or was in need of some arm candy. "I can be myself around you," I would remark whenever Andy and I shared a meal together at a restaurant with some of his buddies.

"That's because you know we're safe." Then taking a bite, he concluded with confidence, "You know we're not interested in trying to get down your pants."

I had been a little shocked at Andy's brash comment in the middle of a public restaurant, made while pouring wine into my glass to go with our pizza, but while I watched Mary sob, I realized he was right. Hanging out with gay men had saved me from the pain and agony that I saw on her face. All I could manage were a few banalities like "I'm sorry," and "I'm here for you if you need to talk."

As the semester progressed, our conversation continued around the office.

"Jenny, now that Tim and I are officially divorced, I want to get back on the market again. I'm tired of being alone. Got any dating advice?" Mary and I were in the middle of a mindless mass-mailing project, but her question hit me like a bomb. I looked up at Mary, dropped the envelope I was holding, and scrambled for an answer.

"I've never dated, so I'm sorry, I can't help you," my voice trailed off with quiet embarrassment; the last word was barely audible. Mary's mouth had dropped open, hanging on her face like a gaping hole. "Does that answer surprise you?"

Now it was Mary's turn to scramble for words. "Yeah," she said, nodding. "I don't understand why someone like you wouldn't date. Is it from lack of interest or..." Mary's voice trailed into several questions, but my mind stopped at this first one. *Of course, no one is interested. I'm a freak of nature. No one wants to go out with a gimp.*

I stared down at the manila envelope in my hands, unwilling to meet Mary's gaze. "Look, dating is not a priority right now. I spend all of my time on my studies, so I really don't have the energy or interest to be in a relationship." I nodded, trying to convince both of us that I was telling the truth. I looked at my watch, creating an out. "I need to go." I grabbed my backpack, raced down the hall and out to the parking lot, avoiding eye contact with everyone in my path. I was on the verge of tears and didn't want anyone to see my pain. Twenty minutes later, safely inside my apartment, I grabbed my cell phone and called the only person who I knew was home, my sister-in-law, Isobel.

"I'm a freak of nature!" I sobbed in the phone, barely able to choke out the words between hiccups.

"You're not a freak of nature, Jenny," Isobel gently soothed.

"Yes I am!" I despaired, feeling my upper lip strain as it curved into a frown.

"Jenny, it's not true."

We sat for a few moments in silence on the phone. I tried to compose myself, but I was heartbroken by the truth that Mary's comment had forced me to confront.

"Who would ever want to date me? I wouldn't even want to date myself. Nobody wants to date a crippled freak!"

"You're not a crippled freak. You're beautiful."

I sat on my bed for a moment, breathing hard, trying to let Isobel's words inside. I wanted to believe that I was beautiful, that I wasn't a freak, but who could ever get over my twisted legs and awkward movements?

"Come on in, Jenny, welcome!"

I walked inside an old college home on the other side of St. Cloud. Ethan, a 20-something from my church, had invited several people over for homemade pasta and movies. I walked inside the door, uncertain what to expect. I knew that Ethan lived in the basement of his uncle's home, but most bachelor pads I had ever seen were disgusting. Dirty dishes filled sinks while dirty clothes littered the floor. Refrigerators housed science experiments whose smell was only second in pungency behind the body odor that permanently lingered in the air.

As I climbed down the stairs leading to Ethan's abode, I struggled to move, grasping at the cinder block walls for support because there was no railing. When

I reached the basement, I saw furniture that was made in the 70s, a TV lying on the floor connected to several wires, and a kitchenette in a corner room. Men that I had never met before were sitting in the basement, presumably Ethan's friends. I walked to the kitchen where Ethan offered me a glass of milk before he got busy making dinner.

As I walked across the living room floor, one of the men sitting on a lounge chair caught me off guard. *"What, are you limping?"*

His words sounded like an accusation, demanding an explanation. I stopped. My eyes stared back into his eyes, which were deep brown and wondering. *Be gracious, be gracious, be gracious, I said to myself over and over again in my head. Some people don't understand that you have a disability. They get confused; be nice...*

"Yes, I have cerebral palsy. I was born like this." *How come I always have to lay my heart on the table just to make others feel comfortable?*

"I'm sorry."

"No, it's okay." I said, shaking my head. "Many people think that I've been in a car accident or had an injury and they don't understand that I have a disability."

He stared at me, listening. "No, that's not what I meant. I'm sorry you have that."

My fingers strangled the glass in my hand. I looked down into the white liquid that lay inside. Everything in me wanted to throw the milk in his face like I had seen Samantha Jones do on *Sex and the City* when her date was rude. How dare he say such a thing? No one had ever offered me pity! I sat on the couch for the rest of the night, dumbfounded by what I had just heard, unsure how to react. Was this how men saw me: a spectacle, a circus act, a freak show, but not a woman? There was no hope of me ever dating if this was what men were thinking as I walked by.

"Andy, has anyone ever offered you pity?" I asked the next day during a phone call, explaining what had happened last night.

"Uhhh...no, not that I can remember."

Even though he couldn't see me, I nodded in disappointment. Andy was my only friend with CP, and unfortunately he couldn't relate to my dilemma.

"Jenny, I think I can't understand you because of the gender difference between us. I haven't had the same experiences as you. Sorry."

"It's okay, Andy." I paused for moment, trying to decide where to take this conversation next. Then, I laid all my cards on the table. I told Andy about Mary asking me why I hadn't dated, my thoughts about being a freak, and the pain I felt each time I had to say the words "cerebral palsy."

Andy listened patiently to everything I had to say and then laid out his opinion. "Jenny, if you don't want to be in a relationship right now because you're too busy with school, that's one thing."

I listened, agreeing.

"But if you're scared to be in a relationship that's another."

" —I can't talk about CP. It's shameful. I can't say the words, 'cerebral palsy' without chest pain. It hurts so much."

"Then I would suggest some counseling."

Counseling—the word seemed foreign to me, and yet fitting at the same time. I wasn't sure how talking to a stranger could possibly change my situation, but at the same time, I was facing challenges that I couldn't overcome without help.

Counseling...I mulled the idea over in my head as the weeks ticked away. Wasn't counseling for weak people? How much would it cost? Where would I go? Did I have to see a "Christian" counselor? Would she make me talk about God? I didn't want to talk about Him! I wanted to talk about me! I hated myself, I hated living in my body, and I hated that I couldn't even admit that I had cerebral palsy in front of anyone—not family, not strangers, not even close friends.

I continued to pick at this glaring problem with saying the phrase "cerebral palsy" like a scab that wouldn't heal. It was a crescendo growing in its intensity, screaming louder and louder: "You need help, you need help!" One afternoon, this anthem reached its peak. Heading into the grocery store, I came face to face with my pain.

"What happened to *you*?" an old woman asked me as I made my way from my car into the store. Her eyes gave me an appraisal as she looked me over, up and down. I watched her looking at me, knowing that my limp was distinct, probably something common among her arthritic peers, but strikingly out of place for a woman in her twenties. Her eyes were almost mad, like I didn't deserve to look as I did, at least not at my age.

The familiar pain started to twist inside my chest as I mustered up the courage to give her an explanation for what she was seeing. Inside, my head was screaming. *I'm so sorry you have to look at me this way. I know I am a shameful being. I am the one to blame for not having a perfect gait.* But, "I have cerebral palsy," was all I could manage to choke out.

"Oh," the woman grunted, disappointed with the boring answer I had given. She turned and walked into the store while I sat in the parking lot, holding my heart in my hands.

Chapter 13

After making a few phone calls, I decided to start seeing a counselor right on campus. The service was free to me because I was a student, and I could go for as many sessions as I wanted. I was also safe from having to talk about God with my counselor. Sure, I could bring it up, but St. Cloud being a state university, I was certain that *no one* was going to get me into a corner and try to "pray me out of this situation." I could talk to God later, but first, I needed to talk about myself.

State your reason for being here. I tapped my pencil against the clipboard to kill time as I waited in the lobby of the counseling office. "Freak of nature" was omitted from the list. "Scared to death to talk about certain topics with the opposite sex" was also mysteriously absent. Embarrassed by my surroundings, I quickly circled *low self-esteem* and looked up to make sure no one was watching. My secret was safe, at least momentarily. If anyone saw me here, I would die of embarrassment and shame.

"Jenny?"

I was startled out of my thoughts, surprised to hear my name being called so quickly. A young blonde woman stood before me, ready to walk me down a hall into a room where we would begin a conversation that I didn't really want to have.

"My name is Monica Jensen; come on back." She motioned me to follow her and I silently obeyed. I wasn't sure what to expect next, but I jumped at the chance to leave the waiting room as soon as possible. Walking down a narrow hallway, Monica led me into a small dark office. I took my seat in a yellow, molded plastic chair while Monica typed a few notes into her computer. I stared up at a painting to my left. A colorful fish swam in the water. It was comforting and allowed my mind to travel somewhere else than I was at the moment. If counseling only involved staring at colorful pictures, then perhaps I would like it, but suddenly Monica swung her chair away from her computer, faced me, and began to speak. "So, Jenny, what brings you here today?"

Stall, stall! Don't get into it just yet, I fretted. *Looking at the painting on the wall is so much easier than what I am about to say.* "I really am straight," I started, "but all of my friendships with the opposite sex have been with gay men."

"Oh?" Monica raised her eyebrows. I doubted Monica was expecting our conversation to begin this way after seeing "low self-esteem" circled on my intake form.

Change the topic! Monica thinks you're weird! "And people think I'm funny too." Monica's eyes started to widen, struggling to follow a conversation that had gotten off to a random start. "In grad school, we have to give these presentations almost every night. Everyone's bored to tears—death by PowerPoint, you know?"

Monica rolled her eyes and smiled with understanding. Glad to have captured her interest, I continued.

"This course happens to be team-taught by two professors, a husband and wife. They thought it would be helpful to have this big black buzzer box that sounds when time is up. It's real annoying, like the one in Taboo." Monica continued to smile, encouraging me to continue. I started shifting in my chair, slowly beginning to feel comfortable and welcome to talk freely with my hands.

"The sound startles me so much that I often kick the table. Pretty soon, the whole room stopped watching the presenters and just started staring at me, waiting for me to jump. People know it's time to be quiet when Jenny Hill kicks the table! I'm a hit!" I smiled with wide eyes, hoping that even in my awkwardness, Monica would think I was a hit too.

"So, you are enjoying graduate school; you've made some good friendships?" Monica probed.

"Yes," I nodded, "I've made lots of meaningful relationships as a graduate assistant. Just the other day, one of the professors brought me into his office and told me about his brother who is blind."

"That sounds interesting."

"It really was."

"Your professor just called you into his office to tell you about his brother?"

I started to lose my momentum, quieting down as I remembered what had happened that day. "No, he wanted to know if I had a disability. He noticed how I always seemed to be so happy but never brought the topic up in conversation."

Monica nodded, encouraging me to say more.

Okay Monica. I'll quit goofing around and get to the good stuff. "He went on to say that professors don't really feel they can ask questions about disability, but that it must be a topic that I enjoy talking about."

Monica nodded, "Was he right?"

"No," I quietly responded, shaking my head. Tears welled up in my eyes while a lump formed in my throat. I tried to ignore it, pushing ahead with what I had to say. I looked away from Monica and back at the picture on the wall to get some relief.

"He was so kind and tactful in his approach. But he couldn't be further off base." I turned and faced Monica, wanting her to understand the intensity of what I had to say next. "I just set my teeth and tried to ignore the pain that was stirring in my chest. The truth is," unable to contain my emotion any longer, I let tears fall from my face, "I really can't talk about the fact that I have cerebral palsy. I can't even say the words." I sat back in my chair and wept.

Monica and I sat in silence in her office for a few moments. I took Kleenexes from the table next to me and sniffled while Monica folded her hands in her lap and thought before she began to speak.

"I think at times we have things that sit uncomfortably in our past. They're uneven," Monica began to illustrate her point, placing one hand slightly over the other. "As you begin to talk, working things out through counseling, the past can sit a little more evenly in your life." Monica slid her hands in place, next to each other forming one even plane.

I crumpled the tissue that was in my hand, staring up at Monica. "So there's hope? I can get better?"

"Yes," Monica said, smiling. "You can get better. I don't know all that cerebral palsy means to you yet, but we'll find out together. Ok?"

"Ok," I nodded. I made an appointment for the following week and headed home.

My next session looked a lot like the first, I checked in and Monica led me down the narrow hall to her office. I stared uncomfortably at the fish hanging on the wall while she typed notes into her computer. As I sat on my molded plastic chair, my stomach filled with anxiety as I thought about having to voice my dreaded two-word phrase. I knew I couldn't hide behind its initials, "CP"; I would have to say the words outright, in their entirety, perhaps several times because today we were going to discuss my silence and my pain. As Monica turned towards me, ready to begin, I held my breath a little, like I was trying to sustain an incoming blow. This was going to be tough, and Monica didn't waste any time getting down to business.

"So, we when we ended our session last week, you said, 'I can't talk about cerebral palsy, I can't say the words.'"

I nodded. *Don't worry, Monica. I remember!*

"What do you feel when you say those words?"

You can do this, Jenny! I began to coach myself mentally. *Just tell her about your physical symptoms.* "I feel a twisting pain inside my chest," I said matter-of-factly.

"Hmmm, that's interesting. Jenny, why do you think those words are so hard to say?"

I thought for a moment, biting my lip. "I don't know."

"Jenny, saying 'I don't know' is a 'cheating' response," Monica said, adjusting her glasses. "It doesn't allow you to process your thoughts fully. I want you to think about the question further. Why do you think saying 'cerebral palsy' is so hard for you?"

I looked back at Monica, wanting desperately to stare at the fish painting on the wall, to break out of this conversation, but chose to stare at my feet instead. This was such a loaded question! So many emotions were swimming around in my head; where did I start? I looked up, sat back in my chair, took a deep breath, and slowly began.

"Monica, I try very hard to do well in school. Before I started college, I had a high school teacher that gave me some great advice."

"What did he say?"

"He said to treat my college career like a full-time job. Put 40 hours a week into it, including class time. Your payment is the grades you receive."

Monica nodded.

I nodded back, glad to see we were on the same page. "I took his advice to heart. It helped me gauge how much time to spend studying on the days when I didn't have much class." I went on to tell Monica about my study room habits, how Dr. Micah's class was traumatizing, and finally about commencement. "College has been a place of success for me," I concluded, "and all that effort has made graduate school pretty easy."

Monica turned her head with curiosity, "Jenny, why did you tell me about academics when I asked you about cerebral palsy?"

Here we go. Just state the facts. Detach from your emotions. "When I walk into a room, people notice that I'm different and they judge me. I have to work extra hard at *something* to prove them wrong." I paused, searching for the right words. "Monica, I'm ashamed of the fact that I have CP. It's an area of my life where I have failed. I figure that if I can show people how smart I am and how perfect my grades are, perhaps they won't see my flaws."

"So, every time you tell someone that you have 'cerebral palsy' you feel like you're flawed?"

"Pretty much." I bit my lip and widened my eyes. A maelstrom of emotions was swirling in me. Part of me wanted to cry openly and part of me wanted to hold back to maintain my composure. I could see that counseling was going to be intense, but if I didn't deal with my emotions now, they would loom over me for the rest of my life.

"Monica, I used to wish that I could rip the words 'cerebral palsy' from the English language," my voice began to crescendo with emotion. I imagined myself ripping an entire page out of a dictionary. "Like maybe if I could delete them, then my condition would also cease to exist." Releasing those words was like exhaling. I felt just a little bit lighter by confessing my desires.

"Words have power, don't they?"

"Yes."

"Have you ever tried to practice talking about cerebral palsy?"

"Vulnerability scares me."

"Say more about that."

"I tried to talk about it once with a couple I met, but it didn't feel right."

"Vulnerability is scary," Monica affirmed. "You have to open up and share a piece of yourself that you may normally keep hidden."

"Why did it feel so uncomfortable? When I shared, I didn't feel like I was well received." I told Monica about how I was so happy to discover people I thought I could relate to, but after sharing part of my story, the couple told me, "Don't be sad; this doesn't bother you now, does it?" Their question couldn't have been further from the truth. The distance between our perspectives made me feel over exposed, and I didn't want our discussion to uncover anything more.

"You have to choose people that you are going to be vulnerable with carefully. Maybe you discovered these were the wrong people," Monica offered.

I squirmed in my chair, considering what Monica had just said. "So, it might not feel so scary with everyone that I decide to talk to?"

"Right. I think if you find people whom you've known for a while, whom you trust to share with, it might still be hard, but I think it will feel more comfortable."

I nodded silently. I hoped that Monica was right. "Can we practice?"

"We can certainly role-play. That's why a lot of people come to counseling. They can practice being vulnerable here in order to build their confidence out in the world."

I sat there, listening. I liked this idea of fortifying my confidence. I wanted to be ready the next time an old lady approached me at the grocery store.

Monica rested her chin in her hand, thinking, her eyes starting to sparkle with connection. "I think some homework that would help you between now and next week is this: find someone who you feel comfortable with and share about your experience with cerebral palsy."

"Ok," I nodded, trying to convince myself that Monica's idea had merit, "that sounds like something I can do."

I drove home to my apartment, lost in thought. Who could I trust to tell my story to? Certainly no one at my church. I loved everyone there dearly, but sharing my story would unravel into too many questions. I didn't want to talk about healing or prayer or my thoughts about God. Counseling was about me, and at the moment, my shame and self-hatred was strangling me, choking out my voice. Who would be willing to hear my whispers, to let me practice saying the words I hated the most?

I wonder if Tom and Katie would listen to me. Katie was the graduate assistant for the GLBT community on campus. Her husband was a youth pastor at another church in town. I had met Katie and Tom through Andy; the two of them had always been so hospitable. I had an open invitation to use their outdoor pool, cable TV, and air-conditioning. Whenever I went over there, I was greeted with their signature chocolate martinis, shaken with strong vodka that burned its way down my throat. We hadn't known each other very long, but perhaps it was long enough, perhaps they would let me be vulnerable. I picked up my cell phone the next day and decided to give it a try.

"Hi, Katie?"

"Hi, Jenny! How are you?"

"I'm good," I paused, feeling like I was about to drop a bomb on an unsuspecting victim. I chose my words carefully, not wanting to scare her off. "Did Andy ever tell you that I was going to counseling?" The phone was silent for a moment; I stood there waiting.

"Yeah, I think he did."

"I'm mentioning it because my counselor just gave me some homework that I'm going to need your help with."

"Ok."

"I ahhh...I..." I started to fumble my words. *Just say the words!* "I have a hard time talking about the fact that I have CP." The words rushed out of my mouth with almost indecipherable speed. I was happy that I saved myself by using the abbreviation for my condition instead of speaking the words in their entirety.

"Okay..." Katie said into the phone, wondering where this conversation was going.

"I need to practice sharing my story with people I trust. So I was wondering if you and Tom and I could have dinner together and I could practice talking about it." Please say yes, please say yes, I silently prayed.

"Thursday sound good?"

I breathed a sigh of relief, grateful that I hadn't scared my friend with my rather odd request. "Sure."

I arrived a few nights later at Tom and Katie's apartment armed with tools. In one hand I held a bottle of wine to complement our pasta dinner. Tucked under my other arm was my thick brown photo album containing my baby pictures; I was hoping it would serve as an effective visual aid. After dinner, the three of us sat around a folding table in their apartment and I began to speak. The first few photos showed a tiny baby lying in an incubator, hooked up to monitors. Ten pages later, a toddler was hiding under the living room coffee table, right hand curled into a fist—a tiny clue that something was wrong. There were photos of me sitting atop a plastic yoga ball during a physical therapy session and others of Gabe, dressed as a skeleton, propping me up in my ghost costume during Halloween, my legs too twisted to stand very long on my own. Then, the photos in my album took a marked turn. Page after page showed me walking up and down a laboratory hallway at Gillette Children's Hospital. Electrodes were taped to my body at weird angles, analyzing my movements. A few pictures later, I was once again in a Halloween costume, but that time accompanied by a full-body cast. Later, I was decorating a Christmas tree. Fresh scars lined my legs.

When the photo album came to an end, I told Katie and Tom about my experiences in high school, my times of loneliness and shame about how my body moved. I told them about how I tried to hide my feelings by earning good grades, but now that school was about to end, I had to deal with my problems, but it was hard because I couldn't seem to say the words "cerebral palsy" without chest pain.

"So that's why I'm here tonight, to practice saying, 'I have cerebral palsy. That's the reason I walk the way I do. I wasn't in a car accident. I didn't pull a muscle. I have a disability, and I'm going to have it for the rest of my life,'" the words came out of my mouth slowly, but surely. I looked up at Katie and Tom, knowing that I was safe. Speaking the truth to my friends, owning the reality of my life made saying the words "cerebral palsy" just a little less painful. Yet, as I sat in their living room, I wondered what they thought. Were the details of my story too much to share? I never would have predicted their response.

Katie turned to her husband, "Tom, is it your cousin that has CP?"

"Yeah," Tom nodded. "But it's a lot more severe than yours, Jenny. He can't speak, and he walks with crutches."

My eyes widened in surprise. With a few simple words, Tom and Katie had begun to change the way I viewed myself. If they had a family member with CP, then my story wasn't shocking or shameful or even unique. It was simply normal, something they had seen for most of their lives, familiar even. If Tom and Katie could handle the truth of my life with neutrality and comfort, perhaps there was hope for me.

Chapter 14

"I did it! I shared my story; I talked to my friends about CP!" I exclaimed with excitement in Monica's office the next week. Monica sat across from me, smiling.

"Good for you, Jenny! How did it go?"

"It went well. I went to my friends' apartment, brought my photo album as a prop, and told my story. Then, when I was done, they told me about a family member who also had CP. Amazing! I never knew they had a connection."

"See? That wasn't so bad, was it?" Monica continued to smile. I could tell she was proud of me for making the effort.

"You're right, Monica," I said, leaning closer to her in my chair. "It was good, but it made me think about other times when I've had to talk about CP, and I was wondering if we could talk about that today."

Monica opened her arms in a welcoming gesture. "Absolutely. Go ahead."

I fidgeted in my chair, getting ready to dig in deep. "I think the reason my conversation with my friends went well is because it was planned. I knew I was going to be talking about cerebral palsy with people I trust, so I prepared myself."

I looked at Monica, trying to see if she was tracking where I was going. "The phrase 'cerebral palsy' means a lot to me; it's personal." I placed my hand on my chest, illustrating what I was trying to say. "People come up to me out of the blue, thinking they're asking an innocent question about the way I walk, and then I have to expose that I have a disability."

"How do they usually react?"

"That's the whole problem," I rolled my eyes recalling how the conversation usually played out. "They're embarrassed for asking when I answer their question, and I'm left hurting because I'd rather not talk about it."

"Do you feel misunderstood?" Monica queried.

"Sometimes," I said, nodding. I told Monica about my experiences with UCP and the physical therapist who didn't think I belonged at their organization. I told her about the woman I met going into the grocery store and then about the man in Ethan's basement who demanded to know why I was limping.

"You know, it's one thing to explain my disability to a curious stranger, but it's quite another when it comes to interacting with the opposite sex, especially when I think about dating."

"Say more about that," Monica began to prod, and I began to feel uncomfortable, but I knew it was her job to steer the conversation, so I followed her lead.

"Well," I thought for a moment while gearing up to spill my guts, "I walk into a room and a man knows right away that I'm not perfect." Monica stared back at me, urging me to go on. "It's just not fair," I said, shaking my head, "It's not a level playing field. They can hide their flaws for at least a date or two, while I have to lay my cards out on the table right away."

"You're right, it's uneven. How would you like it to go?"

I rolled my eyes, trying to be funny, anything to lighten the tension in the room. "Well, my friend Peter says I should meet men sitting down. Great plan, right?"

Monica shrugged, not willing to fully commit to answering my question.

"It would be a good plan," I said, nodding, "but that's not even how I really want to be seen!" My voice got louder as my sentence ended, like I was confessing a deep secret.

"How do you want to be seen?"

"I want men to see me for who I really am!" I looked down at the floor, frantically, searching the carpet for words. My frustration was mounting, I was ready to yell. I clenched my right fist and then extended my index finger preparing to make a list. "I want men to see that I'm nice, kind, intelligent, funny…but they never will because as soon as they see me limp, they're not interested and it's not fair!" I was breathing heavily now, looking at Monica for validation.

Monica gazed back at me and our eyes locked together. "I hear you. I get it. I understand your feelings." The room became quiet with tension. Not sure what to do, I folded my hands, crossed my ankles, and studied the floor.

A few minutes later, Monica began to speak, choosing her words carefully. "Jenny," she began quietly. I slowly lifted my head to the sound of her voice. "Have you ever considered that the men who are unwilling to see beyond your exterior are not the men you want to be with anyway?"

I nodded silently in defeat. You've got me there.

"I'm a little jealous of you, Jenny."

I recoiled. That was the very last thing I expected Monica to say. After all, I was the one going through therapy. "What do you mean?"

"Every woman wants to be seen for her internal beauty. That's what makes relationships last." Monica averted her gaze from me, almost embarrassed and blushing. I stared back at Monica, even further intrigued; every woman had my problem?

"As we age our beauty fades, so at the end of the day, it's what's inside that counts." Where was Monica going with this? Once again I crossed my arms, crossed my legs, and scooted back in my chair.

"It's like you've been given a fast pass." I tried to visualize Monica's analogy as she was speaking. I had been on the Metro in Washington D.C. You could purchase a magnetically lined paper card which opened a gate, letting you ride the train anywhere you wanted to go. "Your relationships get to cut past mere attraction and become founded on the things that matter right away."

I glared skeptically at my counselor. *Whatever, Monica. You're a cute little blonde. You have no idea what it is to be in my shoes.* I had heard enough for the day. "Monica, my head's spinning. Is it okay if we cut things short today?"

"Of course, same time next week?"

"Sounds good."

I left Monica's office and drove across town to Herberger's department store to find a jacket for the spring season. It always seemed weird to go about "normal business" when I had just spent the past hour pouring my guts out to a stranger in a tiny room. My head was crammed full of thoughts after our hour together. Never once had I walked out of Monica's office without feeling wasted, totally ruined to do anything productive for the rest of the day. Why I had chosen this particular moment to purchase a coat, I had no idea, but as I rode the escalator down to the bottom floor of the store, I felt grief welling up in my soul. *I need to get out of here.*

I frantically searched through the racks, looking for a coat that would fit, clumsily tried it on, and then hurried to find a cashier. I mumbled through the transaction and headed to my car as fast as I could. As soon as I got to my apartment, I closed the door, slid down against the wall, held my head in my hands, and wept.

This time I held nothing back. There was no one in front of me asking probing questions. No one to remain composed for. Talking about my disability had uncorked something in me and I needed to pour it out. First, I cried about small things—the fact that I never was able to ride a regular two-wheel bike like the rest of my family, that I couldn't wear high heels, that I never learned to swim. Then, I moved on to grieving over events in my childhood. I cried over the fact that I had an operation, that I had spent time in a body cast and hours in physical therapy. I cried because I trick-or-treated one year in a wheelchair while my brother brought my bucket to the door and asked for candy because I couldn't. I cried over the loneliness I felt in elementary school and the rejection I endured in junior high.

I wept over the fact that I had spent so much time and energy attempting to cope through academics. Where had that left me? I was all alone; perfect grades had gotten me nowhere except deep in a puddle of tears. My unending emotion scared me. Hour after hour I wept, moving from the floor to my loveseat, to the kitchen stool, and eventually into my bed. Was this how it was going to be? Was I going to be a dysfunctional mess for the rest of my life? Eventually, my tears were overcome by exhaustion and I fell asleep.

"Monica, how can I make my emotions stop?" I demanded immediately at our next session. "The amount of crying I'm doing lately, I—I'm afraid I'm not going to be able to do my job or keep it together as a student." I looked at Monica, begging for answers, hoping she could bring relief. "I feel like I'm going to be swallowed up."

Monica remained calm despite my panic. "Emotions generally come and go in waves," she paused, letting her words sink in. "There are times when emotions seem overwhelming, and then they subside for a while before growing in intensity."

I shook my head, despairing a little. "They're so strong. I don't know what to do. I cried all night last week after talking to you. It scared me."

"Don't worry about your emotions 'swallowing you up.'"

I looked at Monica with hopeful eyes, "Why not?" It seemed that where I was headed, I would soon be suffering a similar fate as the Wicked Witch of the West, drowning in a puddle of my own tears on my kitchen floor.

"Because it takes more energy to suppress your emotions than it takes to deal with them," Monica answered. She reached out and took my hand, looking at me in the eyes. "I know you're scared, but it's okay. Sometimes your emotions are going to feel big and overwhelming, but then they'll shrink and subside."

"It's okay to cry?"

"Yes, absolutely. Let yourself feel experience everything that you are feeling inside."

I sat back in my chair, unwilling to take the bait. I hated emotions; they overwhelmed my brain, taking away my power to think and scrutinize my thoughts so I could understand their meaning. I didn't like how much counseling had caused me to feel, but I refused to give up. I couldn't continue to live my life in shame and counseling seemed to be offering a way out.

"Monica, can we talk about my parents?"

"Ok."

"Well, I think part of the reason my emotions scare me is that I've never really accepted the fact that I have CP."

"Go on."

"My parents…" I began to squirm in my seat, not wanting to move ahead, but refusing to stop. *Talking about my feelings is so hard. I hate it!* "They made a decision early on to raise me as if I didn't have a disability."

"Interesting. How does that make you feel?"

How does that make you feel? I mimicked sarcastically in my mind. "Well…on one hand it's good. I think my parents raised me that way because they didn't want me to view my life in terms of my limitations."

Monica nodded, going along with my line of thinking.

"I've accomplished a lot," I continued. "I don't think I would have become the student I am if they would have sat me down and told me I was different."

"And on the other hand?"

This is so painful. "Well, it's just not reality. I have a disability." I looked away from Monica, unwilling to meet her eyes. I was embarrassed of my emotions and I didn't want to show her.

I sat in my chair, trying to compose myself, fighting my bottom lip that was starting to quiver and my top lip that seemed insistent on turning into a frown. "We just never talked about cerebral palsy at home. And um…" I pressed my lips together, trying to keep them from trembling any further. "It's not like I wasn't allowed to talk about it, it just wasn't family norm."

"I see."

I breathed deeply, trying to summon the strength to continue. "I'd get into these situations at school growing up where I came face-to-face with the fact that I had CP, and I felt like I had nowhere to go." I looked down at my hands, searching. "I couldn't talk about it at home; CP didn't exist. What's was I supposed to do? I just stuffed it."

"Can you tell me about one of those situations?"

I don't want to. Behind my conversation with Monica there was another one going on in my head. It seemed to play out like a tug-of-war. After Monica asked a hard question, one side of me would pull back, refusing to answer, and the other side who was determined to become healthy yanked harder, often leaving me in a mess of tears. *Go slowly. You can do this.*

"Monica, when I was in eighth grade, I decided I wanted to be in marching band." I chose my words carefully. "Normally, the middle school had their own band, but the band director was recently fired, so they let the eighth graders march with the high school that summer." *Make it stop, make it stop! Go on, go on!*

"I was a percussionist, so we had extra practices," I explained. "First, I tried playing the cymbals, but you have to hold them straight out," I demonstrated, "and my arms got tired."

"I can see how that could happen quickly."

I nodded with Monica, agreeing. "And what was worse is that when I would turn and crash them together, I would pinch the skin on my stomach and I would come home from practice every night bruised."

Monica winced. "That sounds painful."

"It was, so eventually I switched to playing bells, and they built a special harness for me." I was silent for a moment. "But before all of that was figured out, umm...." Tension rose in my chest. I had never told anyone about what I was going to say next.

"It's okay, Jenny. It's okay if this is hard."

I folded my hands in my lap, trying to compose myself as much as possible before continuing. "I obviously wasn't very good at marching band. Walking is one thing, but trying to march and play an instrument at the same time is another."

I watched as Monica sat in front of me, trying to picture this in her mind.

"So every day, during practice, when the adults weren't around, my classmates would come up to me, pierce me in the eyes, and taunt, 'Are you going to quit?' I would stare back at them, hurt by their words, confused by their question, and...I...said...nothing."

The room was silent once again. I felt some relief, finally giving voice to a secret I had kept hidden.

"Jenny, do you have a close relationship with your parents?"

I nodded. "I tell them pretty much everything."

Monica began to get into her "rephrase" mode. "So, what I hear you saying is you have an honest and open relationship with your parents, you communicate about everything, but when it comes to anything related to CP, you hold back."

"Yep. That's pretty much it."

"Jenny, why do you think you don't talk to your parents about your CP?"

Allowing Monica to sit and question me about painful topics was a little like watching a sad movie. It starts with some foreshadowing, maybe even a few happy moments, and then gradually piques at your sympathies until you're about to burst. Monica had just hit a nerve. I swallowed hard, forcing the lump back down my throat, looking to my left, searching for my fish on the wall, hoping to find comfort, needing an escape.

"I love them, you know," I confessed, looking up, tears were falling from my face.

"I know."

"We never talked about CP as a family, but I always knew it was a painful topic for them, so..." I struggled to talk in the midst of my trembling lips, "...I tried to shield them from my pain. Why should they hurt too?"

Monica brought her hand to her face, covering her mouth. Her eyes were focused, deep in thought.

"Are there parts of your therapy conversations that you would like to share with them, but haven't been able to?"

I nodded, painfully. "I want to tell them about my fears of dating, how many men won't give me a second glance. I need them to validate my fears. I need to know that I don't have to do this alone."

"Ok...so..."

"I'm afraid!" I sobbed. "My mom's going to cry! I don't want to hurt her!"

Monica looked at me with concern before answering slowly. "Well, I'm a mother, and I have to tell you, I would be a very cold person if I didn't hurt when I found out my child is hurting."

I sat in my chair, looking back. What Monica was saying was making sense.

"That's what parents do, they care about their children. Don't be afraid to talk to your parents because of the emotion you fear will stir in them. If they cry, it's out of concern."

I pondered Monica's words for a while before speaking. My parents knew I was going to counseling to grapple with my cerebral palsy, but they knew nothing of my dating fears or how I wanted to talk about CP with them. This conversation was going to be harder than the one I had just had with my friends, but grappling with rejection without my parents' support was proving to be harder still. "Okay," I said, "I'll do it."

My parent's home was only 30 miles from campus, so I met them for lunch the following Sunday after church. We sat together at the kitchen table together like we had done for years. As I plunged my fork into my spinach salad, bringing them up to speed on my counseling sessions, I summoned the courage to say the words I needed. I made eye contact with both of my parents and began, "I've been talking to my counselor about how we never talked about CP at home growing up."

My parents looked back at me, listening.

"I know that I could come with you at any time about anything, but CP was just never a topic of conversation. Why?" I looked across the table; my mom was beginning to lose her composure.

"Jenny, your dad and I sat down at a very early stage and talked about how we were going to raise you."

I stared back in surprise; my parents had never told me this before.

"We made a conscious decision that we never wanted to send the message to you that you were any different than anyone else."

Well it turns out that I am! I hid my anger, taking another bite of my lunch. My mom continued, "We couldn't just sit down and say, 'Now Jenny, there are some things in life that you're never going to be able to do.'" My mom made a patronizing gesture, as if she was patting someone on the back.

"I know," I interjected. "I've met someone like that who I swear had been taken aside and told he was different. It wasn't good. He didn't have a very good view of himself, but...this is so hard," I whispered under my breath, shaking my head.

"I wished you would have raised me differently." As the words fell from my mouth, I imagined that they were the worst that any parent could ever hear. I looked across the table, thinking that my parents were going to explode, but they surprised me, sitting there patiently, waiting for me to finish my thought.

"I mean, take marching band for example. I was climbing up the steps of the bus one day to go to a parade. The kid in front of me didn't know that I was behind him, that I could hear him making fun of me."

I'd captured my parents' attention now as they stared back at me. It was their turn to hear new information.

"He called out, 'You'll never guess who joined marching band...Jenny Hill!' Kids on the bus erupted with laughter like I was some kind of joke."

My dad put down his fork. "You've never told us that before."

"That's my point," I answered back, frustrated. "I never felt like I could. CP wasn't something we talked about at home."

"Well, I agree it wasn't something we talked about much," my dad adjusted in his chair.

"We wanted to raise your confidence at home," my mom began to explain, "so that when people made comments like that they would just go over your head."

I looked at my mom, floored. "Go over my head?" How could she think that I was so clueless? "Well, his comments didn't 'go over my head,' I knew exactly what was going on!" I stared back, waiting to hear what would come next. My frustration was disarmed with a question.

"How do you wish you were raised?" my mom asked gently.

"I'm grateful that you taught me not to view my life in terms of my limitations, but I wish you would have acknowledged that there were going to be some emotional hurdles in my life."

My parents nodded, beginning to see where I was coming from.

"Jenny, you can always come to us," Dad offered. "Is there something you would like to talk about with us today?"

I exhaled, letting all the air in my chest come out of my mouth. I stared down at the table, avoiding eye contract, trying to distance myself from the conversation. "My counselor and I have been talking about dating," I revealed, slowly raising my head. "I'm think I'm scared to date because I'm scared to talk about cerebral palsy." I took another bite of my salad, needing to take a break before continuing. "I'm afraid that as soon as I bring it up, I'm going to be rejected. I know we've never really talked about CP before, but I feel I need to talk about it with you now. I need your support. I need you know that this is really how I feel." I took a deep breath and told them about the man's comments to me in Ethan's basement. My parents listened carefully, but I only made it halfway through before I started sobbing. My mom ran to grab the Kleenex box on the other side of the living room.

Crying uncontrollably, I looked at my dad in the face, searching for validation. "I need to hear you say it, Dad," I cried, "I need to hear you say that some men won't take a second look at me because I have CP."

My dad was quiet for a moment, folding his fingers, bringing his index fingers together in a point underneath his chin. "You're right. Some men won't give you a second look after they see you limp, but you need to realize, those men aren't the ones you want to go out with anyway." I let his words come into me, grateful for his honesty, even though it had been painful to verbalize.

"You also need to realize, that if someone does come along who is interested and you do break up, it wouldn't be because you have cerebral palsy, it would probably be for another reason."

I mulled the conversation over in my mind while driving back to St. Cloud that evening. Talking to my parents had been hard, but I was able to gain some new perspective. On some level I had always viewed CP as my only flaw because it was the one that was most visible, but listening to my dad's thoughts helped me to consider that rejection could actually happen on another basis, like any other *normal* woman; this was very freeing.

For what seemed like the first time in my life, I began to see the possibility that, because of our honest dialogue that afternoon, cerebral palsy could eventually become a topic of conversation between the three of us. With that hope in mind, I went to my counseling session the next day and told Monica I was ready to take a break from the counseling process over the summer.

Chapter 15

My parents own a cabin in Nisswa, MN, that they restored after the previous owner passed away. It's oddly shaped, a cottage made of one long rectangle that faces little Lake Gladstone. Now that I was away at school, I no longer had the luxury of walking in the potato field any time I needed to get away. It was the lake that became my new sanctuary. As a graduate student, I spent the majority of my summer at the cabin: fishing, reading, and riding my tandem bike. After many failed attempts, I had resigned myself to the fact that I was unable to balance a two-wheel bike independently. I lost my balance and fell off every time. To adapt to my specific needs, my parents purchased a tandem for me so that I could join them on their outings along Nisswa's famous biking trails.

Learning how to bike in tandem was somewhat of a process, but my family and I quickly perfected a routine. The front rider mounted the bike and held it in place with their feet firmly planted on the ground. I, in turn, mounted the back seat and placed my feet on the pedals, ready to push. Next, the front rider put their feet on their own pedals and then we were off! I had to sit in the back of the bike as I couldn't seem to balance the bike while pedaling. I also didn't have to worry about my slow reaction time from the back seat because the front rider decided when to start and stop the bike. Riding back-seat tandem is an act of trust because you have no control over your ride; you just pedal, believing the person in front will take care of you.

My particular bike had handle bars that were connected to the front rider's seat, so the shorter the rider, the farther I had to lean forward to grasp the handles. To compensate for this design, I usually tried to ride with the tallest person available. One particular day, I was riding with my uncle Joe, a tall biking enthusiast. After a little communication and successfully executing my mounting routine, we made it through the cabin's wooded drive and out onto the road. After a few hundred feet, we turned and biked on a smoothly paved asphalt trail with trees peeking down, extending their branches to offer shade. We cruised through the trail at a moderate speed, while Joe got used to telling me when to brake and when to pedal until I fell in sync with his rhythm. We pedaled in silence for a few moments while I looked up to see what was in front of me: the dominating image of Joe's back bent slightly over, with a little foliage peeking out of my periphery.

"Make sure you get your head up and look around. That's the best part of biking, enjoying the scenery."

I'm sure it is, I thought, *but I wouldn't know because I'm always stuck on the back of the bike.* "Okay!" I called from my seat, "I'll try!" I tried to peek around the sides, leaning to my right and then to my left. It was no use. The only scenery I was going to see on this trip was Joe's golden yellow bike shirt. I centered myself on my seat, determined to keep pedaling, when something inside of me exploded. Suddenly, overwhelming frustration brewed in my chest; I had ridden on the back seat ever since I was too old for training wheels. I was sick and tired of being dependent, never having the opportunity to take in the beauty that Joe saw every time he whizzed past the world on two wheels. I was angry that I had never told anyone about it.

After my uncle had gone home, I turned towards my parents and let loose in a flood of angry tears, "I want to ride in the *front* seat of my bike!"

My mother tried to reassure me, "Honey, you've tried to do that before, but you couldn't handle it; your muscles, they're too tight, and you couldn't keep your balance."

I looked at my mom, mad that I could recall those memories, wishing they were not part of the story of my life. Didn't they understand? I knew I couldn't ride a "normal" bike, but having to ride with someone else made me feel childish. I wanted them to come up with a solution; my anger demanded that they create an escape.

"Jenny, you've done a great job handling your emotions, and I can't say how I would react in this situation," my dad began, "but there is no need to be dramatic. Just don't focus on it."

I looked at him, pausing for only a moment, before I turned around and headed straight for my bedroom. I closed the door, needing some time alone. The cabin was already small, but it seemed to be shrinking fast. I scanned the floor, looking at my clothes, wondering how fast I could pack them away so I would not have to spend another minute trapped in this conversation. I played my parents' comments over in my head. *Just don't focus on it?!* Not only did that make me angry, but it made me feel confined, like I wasn't even given permission to experience or express the emotions raging inside me while my limitations stared me in the face. I sat down on the bottom bunk. I may have been on hiatus from counseling for the summer, but after what happened, I knew I had to resume my sessions when the school year began. I still had issues that needed to be worked out.

"What is the purpose of anger?" I demanded at my next counseling session. I told Monica what had happened at the lake while riding my bike and the unexpected rage that erupted. "I went from zero to pissed so fast that I got scared." I shook my head, looking for an explanation. "I don't experience anger very often; I don't understand it."

"Anger produces energy in us," Monica affirmed. "It gives us the ability to rise up in order to say and do things that we wouldn't normally."

That's really helpful, Monica, I thought with sarcasm, *especially when your parents tell you to "just not focus on it."* How am I supposed to express myself to them!?

Monica looked at me. She could see I was brewing. "Jenny, you said you were scared of anger. Why do you suppose that is?"

"I don't know," I began, reaching. "It's uncontrolled; it clouds my thinking because the emotion seems to dominate my brain." I shook my head, still confused. "It comes out of nowhere and I don't have an outlet to express it. I feel like it's an emotion that I'm not allowed to have."

Monica raised her eyebrows. "Say more about that."

"I don't think I can."

"Take a minute."

I sat there in my yellow chair pondering, hunched over, staring at the floor, hoping the grains of the carpet would provide some answers. After a minute, I folded my hands and straightened up. "Composed people don't act that way. It goes against who I am."

"And who is that?"

"Someone who tries to be controlled...together...perfect."

"What if sometimes you weren't perfect?"

"Then I would be a failure."

"I see," Monica nodded slowly. "'Failure' is a strong word to call yourself." I shrugged my shoulders in reply. I wasn't going to argue with that one. It was the truth; failure was the enemy that I was fighting against, constantly trying to keep it at bay. "I think there's more to this, but we're at the end of our time today, so let's pick this next time."

The next week when I went to counseling, Monica greeted me and told me that she had gotten a new office. It was further down the dark hallway but ended in a room with windows. I stepped in, looking around. My trusty fish painting that had carried me through my previous sessions was nowhere to be found; my yellow chair had also been replaced.

"What do you think?"

"It's...different," I said, trying to be positive—but I wanted my fish back. What I couldn't ignore, however, was the comfort I found in the sunlight streaming through the windows of Monica's new office. Perhaps this was a sign of hope?

"Have a seat," Monica gestured, pointing towards an orange, retro armed chair. I obediently slid into place, resting my arms on either side of me. "How are you feeling?"

"Ok," I began, "I've been thinking a lot about myself since last week. I've felt frustrated and angry sometimes, and I've thought more about failure."

Monica leaned back in her chair and crossed her legs. "I'm glad to hear you've been processing—that's good. Tell me what you've been thinking."

"Well, I've been thinking that I would have more peace with myself if I accepted the fact that I have cerebral palsy, but if I actually did that, I'd feel like a failure."

"Go on."

This time I sat back in my chair, thinking about people I had encountered with disabilities, people I'd met through United Cerebral Palsy, my volunteer experiences, or interacted with in public. Sometimes it was hard to explain the experience of living with a disability to someone like Monica who didn't, but I was going to try.

"Over the years, I have met other people with CP or other disabilities who are trying to cope, right?"

"Right."

"It seems that most of their approaches to life fall into one of two categories. Some of them have chosen to 'take the bull by the horns' and live their lives fully. Take Christopher Reeve for example; I saw the man on TV, yachting after his injury."

Monica smiled.

"Others seem to only view their lives through the lens of their limitations. They act like victims. I swear, it's as if someone took them aside and gave them a lecture." I waved my index finger as if scolding a child out in the hall. "You're never going to be as good as everyone else, your life is going to present challenges beyond your ability to cope, and living in chronic self- pity is a totally acceptable way to deal with it." I leaned forward in my chair, wanting to emphasize my point, filled with energy, "And they believed it!"

Monica sat there patiently, waiting for me to continue.

"I mean, I feel like I come across as a very competent person—I don't want to have to give that up!" I leaned toward Monica again, hoping she understood.

"I'm afraid that if I accept my disability, I'll become a victim and that's not who I want to be."

"You do come across as a competent person..."

Whew! Thank God!

"... and it's good that you do not want to give up that persona," Monica affirmed,

I'm glad you agree with me.

"...but accepting your disability does not have to mean that you become a victim, it can simply mean that you feel comfortable talking about this area of your life."

I stared at Monica, arrested by this new line of thinking. Was it actually possible to accept my CP and not be a victim? I was still skeptical. In my mind, there were only two teams: those that ignored their disabilities, living successful lives, and those that were overwhelmed by them, the failures.

"I've never thought about that before," I said, slighting brushing the suggestion off. "Here's how I see it," I continued, pointing my finger. "I've worked *my whole life* to compensate for the fact that I have CP. I studied hard in school, got perfect grades, and I try to present myself like I'm the smart one; I'm the one with all the answers." I could feel myself beginning to ramp up.

"And why do I do it?" I looked back at Monica, daring her to guess, but giving her no time to respond, "I do it so that other people see that I have some *redeeming* quality in me instead of the mess they see when I walk into a room." I quieted my voice. "If I have to accept that I have CP, then I have to acknowledge that I have *failed*." It felt good to release the words, angry as they were. It was so much easier to tell Monica than tell my parents. She didn't take it personally; she didn't cry. I was her client; I wasn't her kid.

"Tell me more about that," Monica probed.

I looked back at Monica and in that moment made a decision to tell her about my teenage heartbreak. I had never once told anyone about Ian Parker since I had moved to St. Cloud. I had determined before I started counseling that this was not going to be about God. But if Monica was ever going to understand why admitting that I had CP was the same to me as admitting failure, she was going to have to understand this part of my past.

I started at the beginning. I told Monica about my church experiences, my unique relationship with Ian Parker, and the many times that I had prayed for healing individually and at the hands of others. Even though I had never voiced these events before, telling them to someone who was not part of the church felt safe. Monica, I was sure, was not going to judge me, and she sure wasn't going to concoct some theological Band-Aid to explain why I wasn't healed.

"Do you think your relationship with Ian Parker was all bad, or were there some good consequences that came out of your interactions?"

The long-term effects Ian had on my life and the events surrounding it were so profound. I had never stopped to consider if any of it was "good."

"It wasn't all bad," I finally decided. "It was nice to have someone's attention." I shrugged, "Most people wouldn't give me the time of day, but he seemed to care about my situation and at least try to offer a solution—that in itself was unique." I mused a little further, wondering how I should continue. "But I didn't like the fact that I was on stage with an auditorium full of people praying for me; that was too public."

"Oh," Monica gasped, quickly bringing her hand up to her face, trying to cover her mouth and conceal her reaction. Her eyes widened with realization of the situation.

Oh no. I thought, disappointed. *Monica thinks I'm a freak.*

I started to backpedal—trying to clarify. "You didn't get that from what I told you," I said, shaking my head, "that this all happened on stage in front of hundreds of people?"

I could see Monica was embarrassed by her show of emotions. "No."

"What did you think?"

"I thought that this happened quietly in the back of a church, someone just prayed for you."

That would have been ideal. "My relationship with God changed after that," I continued, "I don't see Him the same way." I struggled to form this sentence.

I couldn't put words to what I had experienced as a Christian or was attempting to describe, yet Monica correctly reflected, "It sounds like this experience has shaken your faith and changed the way you view yourself. Hmmm...."

Hmmm...indeed. There was going to be so much to ponder on my own this week.

When I wasn't at school or out with friends, I spent my time in my little one-bedroom apartment just outside of St. Cloud, that my friends had affectionately named "the dollhouse." Efficiently packaged inside three little rooms was everything a girl needed: direct entry from the outside, convenient when bringing in groceries; a stacker washer and dryer tucked into the corner of my bathroom; and a generous kitchen counter which doubled as a kitchen table, leaving my living room free for relaxing.

Gabe had bought me a TV as a graduation present after I finished high school. It was a large, flat, square box that sat on top of an old desk brought home from the cabin. My parents remodeled their home after becoming empty nesters, and I became the recipient of their iconic early 1990s dusty blue furniture set: one loveseat and one wing-back chair.

Living alone, I often found myself turning on the TV to bring some comforting noise into my home. The Saturday morning following my counseling session, while I was cleaning my apartment, a news anchor was interviewing a local Minnesotan who had been injured in a car accident as a child, leaving him a quadriplegic. Miraculously, he had become an award-winning yoga instructor highlighted on NBC's Today Show. I took a break from cleaning my floor for a moment, sat down on my loveseat, and turned up the volume.

"You always hear people in society say, 'she overcame her disability by...' fill in the blank. I think those messages are well intended, but they're also pervasive." I leaned further into my TV—glued to the words coming out of this man's mouth. "It's an unrealistic expectation to think that people with disabilities should somehow overcome their challenges." *Absolutely!* "I will never overcome my paralyzed body...what I've had to learn is how to live well within it." As the interview faded into a commercial, I ran into my bedroom to Google the name of the man being interviewed. I was eager to hear more, hungry for a mentor to come alongside me and explain this inner turmoil that I had been experiencing these last six months during counseling. He wasn't playing on the successful denial team nor was he championing the victimized failures. He had found a way to live somewhere in between, and this was the destination I was longing for!

I quickly found a radio interview he had given the previous year and started to listen. "I had to grieve the loss of my fully functional body before I could accept who I was." *Oh God!* I gasped, sitting up in my chair. His words brought me deep understanding and camaraderie for the gut-wrenching process that had been taking place in Monica's office week after week. *That's what's happening to me!* I was shocked and frightened by this new revelation, yet oddly comforted at the same time: it so clearly explained my denial, followed by periods of deep sadness and episodes of anger. It gave definition to this game of mental ping-pong that was starting to play out in my head. Could I accept my disability and not become a victim? Could I live in reality, yet keep my disability in a healthy perspective? Could "acceptance" look the way Monica had described in her office—feeling comfort in talking about CP, but not making it the sole conversation of my life?

Needing to ponder without distraction, I turned on the faucet in my bathroom and filled my tub. Warm water always seemed to calm my body, bringing relief to my tightened muscles. I added some bubble bath and slid in, letting the water embrace me. I stared straight ahead at my washer and dryer sitting in the corner of the room. Folded white dish towels sat on top. "I felt like I was waving a white flag of surrender." More words from the interview swirled in my head. This was something, I realized, that I too needed to do. "I can never be perfect," I said aloud in my tub. "I can't ever be all that society wants me to be," I shook my head, growing more confident. "I cannot overcome my disability." Although I was nestled underneath a blanket of bubbles, I felt like I was standing before a crowd at an AA meeting, admitting my short-comings and announcing my victories. "It doesn't mean that I'm a failure; it doesn't mean that my body is shameful," I began to smile. The two sides were coming together; my mind was finally beginning to accept this well-bargained agreement. "It just means that I accept and talk about the fact that I have cerebral palsy and will have it for the rest of my life!" I nodded my head, confident of my decision. I closed my eyes, sliding back against the tub. I pictured my mind standing in a doorway, greeting my disability like two friends reconnecting with each other after a long time apart. In an embrace, they happily shook hands while my mind said, "Welcome to Jenny's body, cerebral palsy, I understand you're here to stay!"

As I lay in bed that night, for the first time in a long time I began to feel whole. Something significant had shifted inside me, like a joint being popped back into place, relieving the pressure and alleviating my pain. And yet...my mind flashed back to the scene in Monica's office last week, as she brought her hand to her mouth, unable to maintain her composure, shocked by the details of my past. Who could ever understand what had happened to me? I couldn't; there were simply no words to describe the pain that I felt towards God.

Satisfied that acceptance of CP meant I no longer had to live with denial, self-hatred, shame, or silence, I was willing to quit while I was ahead. It would be nice to have a restored relationship with God, but that just wasn't possible. His decision to withhold healing had scarred me for life; there was no going back. I had just accepted that my physical walk was going to be marked by a limp forever. My spiritual walk, I decided, would have to limp forward as well. God would continue to withhold His healing from me, and I would resent Him for it. It was dysfunctional, but it was a relational stumbling block I was willing to live with. There was no more need for counseling; it was time to move on. Judging from her reaction, Monica couldn't help with this problem. It was too big, too weird, and had no solution.

Chapter 16

The subject line of the e-mail in my inbox read: *"Are you still around?"* *That's an appropriate question,* I smirked, sitting back in my office chair. It had been nearly a year since I had last seen Monica. During that time, I had busied myself with classes, homework, and internships. One of my internships was with Bryon Anderson, a man I had gone to church with for the last six years. He was employed at a local middle school and had spent time mentoring me. I looked up to him as a role model, both as a media specialist and as a Christian. He wrote me a strong letter of recommendation when I started applying for jobs. A few months prior, I had signed a contract for a permanent job in the fall, working at an elementary school that was closer to the Twin Cities of Minneapolis and St. Paul. I had purchased a town home close to my new job but was currently working at a temporary campus job in the Miller Center, waiting for the school year to begin. It was mid-August; I only had one week left.

I clicked on the message and began to read. My friend Daniel who worked at St. Cloud State University wanted to know if we could meet on my last day at the university. "I'm free for coffee on Friday. I'd love to see you!" I responded.

The Miller Center contained a coffee shop that was a mere few hundred feet from my cube. Stainless steel chairs sat around smooth tables made of granite. The baristas were always pleasant to talk to, happy to serve coffee, cookies, or the occasional bowl of soup. That particular morning, I chose a caramel smoothie topped with plenty of whip, which Daniel insisted on paying for. Daniel was always generous, and I had enjoyed getting to know him as he started working in Beth Carlson's office when she became Dean of Students. He had visited my church once; I knew he was a Christian.

At a table near the center of the room, I sipped my smoothie slowly and my teeth grew cold while I listened to Daniel talk about what was happening at the College of Education. I told Daniel about my new job that was starting in a few weeks. His eyes grew wide, excited to hear of my future plans.

"There's a really good church right by your work. I think you'd like it—Church of the Open Door."

I tilted my head to the side, thinking, "I think I've heard of it; they've been in the news lately, right?"

At my mention of the news, Daniel withdrew, his eyes growing deep and dark as he nodded gravely. "Their receptionist drowned last month in the Temperance River."

"That's right!" I said wide-eyed, slamming my drink down on the table. "I grew up in the same hometown as her family. It's so sad!"

Daniel nodded. "I was just on vacation there recently. There's a sign that says 'no swimming,' but the water looked so cool and inviting."

I closed my eyes, trying to picture it. "Do you know how it happened?"

"I guess she was helping out with a camp for teenagers who had decided to go rock climbing for the day," Daniel took a sip of his coffee before continuing. "They all decided to cool off in the water afterwards."

I leaned in, not wanting to know the details, yet curious at the same time. "The water at that part of the river is shallow. Julie was actually sitting down in it with her back leaning against a rocky ledge. One of the teenagers, Andrea, was standing up near Julie when, all of the sudden, she slipped and found herself caught in the current."

My eyes began to widen.

"As she passed, Julie grabbed her and tried to hang on to both the rocks and Andrea, but she couldn't hang on to both," Daniel grew quiet. "By the time they found the bodies downstream, they were both dead."

We sat in silence for a moment. The image of two bodies floating lifelessly drifted through my mind. I imagined screams of shock and disbelief, ambulance workers arriving in vain, followed by waves of inconsolable pain.

Daniel interrupted my thoughts, returning our conversation to Church of the Open Door. "The pastor there is Dave Johnson. I think you'd like him."

"Oh?"

"He's a really good teacher.... He's kind of a firecracker!"

Firecracker, huh? I wonder what that means... "Ok, I'll check it out. Thanks for the recommendation!"

"You bet. I wish I could go too. I really love that church."

Growing up, I was used to small churches where growing families sat in pews and knew everyone in the congregation. Personal contact information was listed in the bulletin or you could talk to "Susie" afterwards about the bake sale and everyone knew who "Susie" was without introduction. I was used to worship that was "unplugged," usually with a local high school student in the back playing the drums. The pastor stood outside the church, shaking hands with his congregants, following a sermon clearly outlined in the bulletin and filled in with dry humor.

Church of the Open Door was none of those things.

Walking into the sanctuary was like walking into a large auditorium at a university, complete with a balcony. Almost 3,000 people attended every weekend, sitting in movie-theater- style chairs, singing along with worship led by professional recording artists, and listening to sermons delivered by a tag team of pastors who were unlike any I had heard before. Like Daniel had said, the senior pastor was Dave Johnson, an energetic man in his fifties who seemed to possess a deep understanding of theology. His "partner-in-crime" was a younger man, Steve Wiens, who had a complementary style, different from Dave that usually incorporated photography and included real-life application. But the list of pastors didn't end there. Open Door had a whole list of pastors on their website that worked at the church and oversaw various ministries, including a group called 20-Somethings that I quickly joined.

One Monday night at 20-Somethings, Pastor Brad Friedlein tossed out the customary ice-breaker question to us as we gathered around white tables, "Alright, before we start tonight, I want everyone at your table to go around and discuss your relationship with God. How has it progressed? Has it gotten better or worse over the years?"

Brad's question took me by surprise and hit me hard. *This is going to be a painful conversation.* I rolled my eyes, turned my chair, and faced my tablemates. Many of them were quickly wrapping up conversations, smiling and happy. I was jealous; the anticipation of answering Brad's question had clearly been less of a trigger for them as it had for me.

"I'll start," the young man to my left offered. We all nodded. "I went through a rebellious period in my walk with God," he began. "I was raised in a Christian home and had Christian parents who loved and supported me. I grew up in the church, but when I left home and went to college, things started to go downhill."

"Sounds like me," another young man said, chiming in.

"Now, things have changed. I am out of college, working, and I realized that I've made some poor choices in the past. Overall, I'd have to say that as I walk with God, my relationship has gotten better over the years, not worse."

Sorry, I can't say the same, I thought to myself.

Another young adult spoke up, "I'd have to agree with you. My story is the same. In my middle school years, I didn't see a need for God, but my friends kept inviting me to youth group and finally I went. I started to see the need for a personal relationship with God and eventually I asked him into my heart to be my God and Savior. My relationship has also steadily improved over the years."

Must be nice, I mentally observed. Now it was time for the woman directly across from me to share her story. I turned toward her, hoping we would have something in common.

"I've always just loved God," she began. "My dad was a pastor and I went to church every Sunday. I am studying to be in ministry full-time. I want to spend the rest of my life serving Him." She shrugged as everyone around the table seemed to applaud. "I never had a period in my life that I can remember when I wasn't walking with God."

Slowly, one by one, each person around the table took a turn describing the direction their walk with God had taken since they had become Christians. While some admitted to backsliding, everyone at the table said that their relationship with God had either remained steady or had gradually improved over the years. There seemed to be camaraderie at our table of people who understood what it was like to grow in their love for God—everyone except me, and I was the last to speak.

I began to fidget in my chair; what I was about to say was going to be out of place with this crowd. From what I had seen, no one sitting there had a disability, and after hearing their stories, no one had spoken of heartbreak, devastation, or shame. I folded my hands, swallowed hard, and began to speak, barely bringing myself to meet their eyes. "I used to have a very close and special relationship with God," I started. "I'm not going to go into detail here, but I happen to have a condition called cerebral palsy." I stopped speaking for a second to take in their reactions. Their happy conversation tone had changed to stares and silence.

I knew this was going to be uncomfortable...for everyone. "When I was young, I asked God to heal me and it didn't happen. That changed our relationship." I stopped for a few moments, blinking. *I don't think I've ever really said that in public before!* "I don't have loving, affectionate feelings for God. I simply respect and obey Him. My relationship with God hasn't gotten better over the years; it's gotten worse." I looked up again, hoping I hadn't lost everyone's attention. The woman across from me was staring down into her lap. The guys were distracted, looking to friends at other tables. No one had anything to offer.

Just then, Brad started speaking from the front, wrapping up our discussions. The night went forward, but I was left behind, lost in thought. *No one understands me.* I had tried to use vague terms when I shared with my tablemates so I didn't scare anyone, but it was no use. They may not have held their hands over their mouths and gasped like Monica, but their collective silence had spoken volumes. As I took in their reactions, I realized that my relationship with God had some serious problems; the internal pain that had been building in me had reached a point that I could no longer ignore.

Chapter 17

Just like I had done as a child at my desk, I had carved out a place in my townhome, "the book nook," to sit down and read. The "nook" was a small, oddly shaped loft that was nothing more than a truncated hallway with a railing. But where some might see an inefficient use of space, I saw opportunity. Two bookcases were added to my nook shortly after I moved in, along with my dusty blue wing-back chair left over from my apartment. I found a triptych depicting a bookstore that I hung on the wall to fill up white space. After a long search, I added an old wooden card catalog from an antique store in St. Cloud—the prize possession of any librarian.

It was in my book nook where I sat down to read a study by Beth Moore. Beth had risen from the ashes of childhood abuse to become a nationally known teacher of the Bible. After what had happened at 20-Somethings, I knew I needed to focus on my relationship with God, so I started the only way I knew how, trying to be a "good student" by reading the Bible every day. I had heard many people describe that completing one of her Bible studies was like finishing a college course. Needing something less intense, I had picked up her 90-day personal study at a local Barnes and Noble. Each daily lesson was only a few pages long with one question and space to write an answer at the end.

This particular study was called *Jesus, the One and Only*, examining the life of Jesus from His birth in Bethlehem through His death on the cross. I found Beth's writing style to be very inviting, drawing me in, until I came to the part of the story where Jesus was performing miracles. *Why couldn't that have been me, God?* I'd ask in my mind, afraid to voice my complaint aloud. I read the story of the man at the pool of Bethesda before turning to my Bible's study notes. "Jesus walked by several crippled people in order to get to this man. When He got there, He asked 'Do you want to get well?' Some people don't actually want to be cured from their diseases." The last sentence floored me. Clearly it had been written by someone who hadn't been sick a day in their life. *Why did I have to be one of those you passed by? I wanted to be healed with everything I had!* I closed my Bible, breathing heavily at the sound of my thoughts, unable to continue my lesson for the day.

A few days later, I opened my book and continued to read. At the end of the day's study was the question "Why should we praise God?" I picked up my pen to write, pressing it into the page until the ink began to seep through. "We should praise God because He is *holy*," I said in a high-pitched whiny voice as I wrote.

Normally, attending church, praying to God, and reading the Bible were uneventful for me, but when it came to the topic of healing, I felt as though there was a nagging woman inside me, bitter, constantly shaking her finger at God. *How am I supposed to love You when I don't even understand You?* I'd argue in anger each day during prayer. I waited for a response, but none seemed to come.

I hate the fact that You're sovereign, I confessed another day during prayer while reading about Jesus. I had come across another story of miraculous healing during my study and it had made me angry. *You get to sit up there making all the decisions with total disregard for what's going on down here, and I'm supposed to just go along with it.* I found myself waving my finger in the air, hoping it would further prove my point. *You should have healed me 12 years ago when I asked You the first time...I AM RIGHT!!*

"I'm right!" I found myself snapping at God while driving in the car. "You made a mistake! You had it in Your power to heal me when I asked, and YOU DID NOTHING!!

Satisfied that I had made myself clear to the Almighty, I turned up the radio and continued on my way.

My rage continued to simmer below the surface as my first year of teaching ended and the year faded into the summer. No one knew about the nagging woman in my head or the ongoing argument I was determined to win with God. Perhaps my relationship with Him would always be marked with a limp, but I felt I had every right to hold a grudge for as long as I wanted, especially after the phone rang one afternoon that summer.

"Hello?"

"Hi, Jenny, this is Gina from church back in St Cloud."

"Hi! It's great to hear from you!"

"—What are you doing right now?"

I grew suspicious at the abruptness of her question. "My mom's here at my house and we're doing some spring cleaning. Right now we're cleaning my oven. Why?"

"I'm afraid I don't have very good news."

"Okay..." I held my breath, wondering what Gina was going to say next.

"Bryon Anderson died last night."

"What?" I found myself grappling, trying to put together the words I had just heard. "How, Gina? The motorcycle?" I closed my eyes, picturing Bryon showing up at Vacation Bible School in the summer, looking cool on his black bike. He had always worn a helmet, but you could never be too sure....

"No, it was his heart."

I sat down in my living room, gripping my cell phone close to my ear, trying to understand how my mentor had died so suddenly. Unknown to me, Bryon had been living with a heart condition since birth. It limited his involvement in sports. *We had more in common than I realized.* Gina told me how he had been mowing the lawn one evening and then decided to spend some time Nordic Track skiing. Meanwhile, his wife and kids drove over to a friend's house for pizza. He was going to shower and meet them later, but he never showed up. His wife found him in the bathroom, rushing to hide the body so the kids wouldn't have to see.

"Wow! I had no idea..."

"Joy and Bryon struggled with infertility, you know."

"No, I didn't."

"It took them several years to get pregnant; their kids are young.

I sat on my couch, breathing into the phone, unsure how to react. My mind raced back to four years ago when Bryon's oldest son, who was in kindergarten at the time, told me about a cat's retractable claws and the physical characteristics of Gila monsters at a petting zoo during VBS. He wowed me with his intellect while Bryon sat by him, encouraging his curiosity. "He needs a daddy..." I muttered under my breath. Gina gave me the time and date of the funeral, I thanked her for calling, and then I hung up. Too mad to cry, I pointed my finger once again at God and continued my argument. *I hate that You think You can do this just because You're God. You made another mistake!* I held my finger in the air for a second, letting it linger.

The day of the funeral was dark and gloomy. *Fitting,* I grumbled as I found a parking spot. Bryon's funeral drew so many guests that it couldn't be held at the little church we had attended together for years. Instead, it was at the biggest venue in town. As I stood in the reception line, waiting to greet Bryon's wife, a friend spotted me and asked, "How are you doing?"

I looked at him, evaluating if he was a good enough friend to handle the truth. I was sick of telling people the half-honest answer of "I'm fine" when I really wasn't. The crucible of tension stirring in me since Brad posed that loaded question at 20-Somethings had reached its zenith and I couldn't contain it any longer. It irked me that I served a "loving" God who also turned a deaf ear to little girls who wanted to be healed and took 42-year-old daddies away from their children.

"Well, if I was Bryon, I would be waging my finger, yelling at God right now," I answered flatly. My friend raised his eyebrows, taken off-guard by my response. "I'd grab Him by the collar and explain, 'I have a wife and kids down there. You send me back! You send me back!'" My friend, who was usually overflowing with words, stared at me, dumbfounded. I just stood there, annoyed, holding my sympathy card in one hand and my purse in another, waiting for a response.

"I...I...People respond in all different ways...We all grieve differently...That's one way to feel, I guess...."

"I guess."

The line moved forward quickly after that, and I soon found myself face-to-face with Bryon's widow. She hadn't slept for days and it showed. Her hair was frazzled and it appeared that tears had permanently stained her cheeks. She whispered as she greeted people, her throat dry from talking.

"I'm so sorry, Joy," I said as I held out my hand to shake.

She looked at me and frowned with sadness. "Thanks, Jenny." I held her hand, looked into her eyes and nodded, but inside I was shaking my head. *Why God? Why?*

I was still asking God why, telling Him about His "mistakes" in my life and His "misuse" of power as I sat in a chair at a mid-sized metropolitan church between my mom and my sister-in-law Isobel's mom, April, one Friday evening, Labor Day weekend. April had invited the two of us to come along with her to a Beth Moore simulcast where she was speaking on the topic of desire. Even though Beth's study on Jesus had sparked quite an argument with God, I still liked her as a teacher and decided to attend.

"We are motivated by what we *want*," Beth stressed with a southern drawl as she clenched a perfectly manicured fist.

No kidding. I squirmed in my seat, realizing Beth was right.

"What is the different between a want and a desire?" I sat a little farther forward, listening. This was a good question.

"A want is something you feel you'd like to have for a short period of time. You want something for a season and then you want something else in another," Beth paused before continuing. "A desire from God is something you want in season and out, year after year. It doesn't matter your financial situation, where you live, or who you're with, you hold this thing in your heart." *I know what that is.* I wished I could pull up a chair and tell my story directly to Beth. I wanted to tell her how I longed for healing as a child and, as an adult, I still held that grief in my heart. If my deep desire for healing was really from God, how could He choose not to act?

"If God hasn't granted a deep desire of your heart, it isn't that He has forgotten about you."

I tilted my head for a second squinting my eyes, trying to grasp what Beth had just said. *God hasn't forgotten about me?* I wrote those words down on the paper, trying to ponder their meaning. I couldn't accept this, not yet, but her point caused the nagging woman in my head to pause long enough to consider this new point of view. I had always pictured God sitting up in heaven making decisions about my life without me in mind at all. I assumed that at least part of the reason He neglected to heal me was so that He could arrogantly demonstrate His sovereign reign in my life in a way that would beat me into submission. My permanent limp was an exclamation point on a sentence that simply read: *I'm God, and you're not!*

"Pay attention, something is up! He is at work in your life! If He has withheld a desire from you, it's either because His glory or your destiny is at stake."

My destiny is at stake. I shifted in my chair, uncomfortable and yet at ease with the words I had just heard. The possibility that my destiny, my very life, had something to do with God's decision to withhold healing went against everything I had previously thought, but I allowed the idea in, just a little. I wanted to hope that God cared about me, that He hadn't forgotten who I was. Most of all, I wanted to believe that He hadn't ignored the entire struggle that I had faced for the past twelve years. As I sat in my seat, I entertained the idea that perhaps God was actually behind the scenes working to weave the threads of my story together into something that brought Him glory and held genuine purpose for me.

I sat in the car on the way home, simmering. There were so many emotions in my head that I wanted to share with my mom and April, but I couldn't, at least not yet. What was going on in my heart was private; it was just between God and me. I wasn't sure where to focus my attention or how to mask the spring of thoughts welling up within my soul, so I tried to focus on what April was saying.

"You know, Dave Johnson's written a book," April looked at me, peering through the rearview mirror.

Here we go. I had only been working as a librarian for a short time but had quickly learned that the profession was sometimes like being a priest or a bartender: people openly and spontaneously confessed. "I wish I was a librarian," I would most often hear from older women who felt it was too late for a career change; "I'm writing a book," would pour forth from the mouths of the most unsuspecting characters; and of course, who could ignore the seemingly constant book recommendations? "Have you read this book? No!? How could you not!? You just have to! I know you'll love it!" Sometimes I appreciated these little pieces of advice, unsolicited as they were, but often I found them ignorant. People seemed to easily forget that like good food and movies, everyone has their own tastes. Today, however, April had whetted my appetite.

"He has?" I asked in surprise. "Yeah! It's called *The Subtle Power of Spiritual Abuse*. I read it. It was very helpful and very good."

Spiritual abuse, the phrase haunted me, resonating with clarity. *I think that's happened to me. I think those are the words I couldn't find when I was trying to tell Monica about praying for healing.* "Thanks, April. I'll look into it." I wanted to read Dave's book, curious, if nothing else, about what the pastor of my church had to say.

As soon as April dropped me off, I ran up to my bedroom, knelt down by my bed, and began to pray, eager to spill out what was inside of me. "God, I want to thank You for Your sovereign will in my life." I couldn't believe the words I was saying as they fell out of my mouth. I never thought I would be thankful, but if God's plan was better than mine, I'd rather follow His.

"I thank You that You are not in heaven making decisions about my life without me in mind. I know now that You've not forgotten about me; You've not turned Your back in ignorance." As I knelt there praying, I thought about how my sinister, power-hungry picture of God could change to God who was thoughtful and tender. Now it was time to say the hardest words.

"God, I understand that I'm going to have cerebral palsy for the rest of my life, and You're not going to take it away. So, I ask that You would use this struggle for Your glory," I laid my heart out. God's glory was my only hope. If He couldn't use my struggle, then the last half of my life had been a waste. "I don't even need to see how You are using it," I said, shaking my head with my eyes squeezed shut, hoping this would make a difference, "but I trust that You will work all things together for good in my life. I will never fight You over Your decision to withhold physical healing from me again." I opened my eyes and exhaled deeply. The nagging woman inside my head that was constantly complaining about the fact that I wasn't healed, waving her finger in indignation, finding fault with the sovereignty of God, was finally silent.

Chapter 18

New to the working world and single, I found that my calendar was frequently open in the evenings. I had been so used to studying every night while in school that it felt awkward coming home to...nothing. My job as an elementary school media specialist satisfied my daily need for human interaction, but I wasn't sure how to spend the rest of my time outside of work. At certain moments the quietness of my house greeted me like a friend, offering rest at the end of a draining day. Other times, I experienced the stillness of my house like someone giving me the cold shoulder, haunting me with the fact that I was still single, and reminding me that I was all alone. I needed something else to add to my calendar.

Open Door soon launched a mentoring program, asking for young adults to attend church on Wednesday nights with students in middle and high school. After a successful interview and background check, I found myself attending training in the same room where 20-Somethings was normally held. After a long morning of various speakers, Steve Wiens was scheduled to speak on adolescent development.

I rolled my eyes in frustration. "I could teach this session," I said to the girl sitting next to me who was also a teacher.

"I know, right? We do this for a living." She shrugged with optimism, "Maybe we'll learn something new."

"I hope so."

Like his sermons, I found this mini teaching session to be engaging. There were short video clips from a movie I had never seen called *Thirteen* to go along with an outline in our binders detailing the developmental milestones teenagers hit. The information was a review, dovetailing what I had learned when I took *Human Growth and Development* at St. Cloud State. I took the course from a woman named Dr. Jay who wore printed animal T-shirts every day and continually told us of her research interests in death and torture. She was unforgettable; her course was not. After reading a 700 plus page textbook, I learned that the arc of human life was quite simple: we're born, develop through the early 20s, and hit a "peak" for a very short time before we reach senescence. It's all downhill from there.

One day, you wake up to discover you can't read the Perkin's menu any longer and the next you find yourself getting fitted for hearing aids. Not long after, you end up taking the proverbial dirt nap. Nothing was too striking about that, which is why the next words out of Steve's mouth struck me like a slap in the face from someone you love.

"The teenage years are a time where you're so focused on fitting in."
Tell me about it.

"You go to school, wearing the wrong T-shirt, someone calls you 'fat,' and you never wear the shirt again."

"I wish it was just a shirt," I muttered under my breath as my mouth hung open. I suddenly found myself blindingly angry at Steve for using such a provoking example and mad at the idea that some people had the luxury of simply changing themselves in order to fit in while I was still stuck with a permanent limp.

You have been cool your whole life. I sat back and judged the man in front of me that I hardly knew. *You run marathons; you speak in front of thousands every weekend; you're married with three boys...You have no idea what it's like to be different, do you?* I looked down at the table, upset. I was deeply disappointed at the painful reminder that I hadn't fit in high school and even more discouraged that the pastor in front of me could never understand.

"Spiritual abuse is a real phenomenon that actually happens in the body of Christ... What is spiritual abuse? How does it occur? Are you a victim?" I read the opening words of Dave Johnson's book that I had just gotten from the library. His questions intrigued me; I wanted to know more.

"Spiritual abuse occurs when someone is treated in a way that damages them spiritually." *Oh God!* I gripped the book tightly in my hands, reading the definition over and over again. I thought about the prayers that Ian had prayed over me on stage which led me to believe that I was "foul and nasty"; I thought about how my hopes were crushed when he promised a miracle that never came.

"As a result, their relationship with God—or the part of them that is capable of having a relationship with God—becomes wounded or scarred." *I need help!* I began to breathe heavily, confronted with the truth of these words. *But not now!* I picked up the book and threw it under my bed, just like I had done with *Joni* in seventh grade. If Dave was right, if I had been abused, then the help I needed was going to be painful, and it was a pain that I was not ready to face.

"Reminder of Library Materials Due." I clicked on the e-mail to see what I had out from the library. *The Subtle Power of Spiritual Abuse.* I clicked "renew," then closed my laptop. I wasn't ready to read Dave's book, not yet.

"Miss Hill, why do you walk like you're galloping?" I looked into the smiling brown eyes of the little boy who was sitting with his classmates on the first day of school. Even after all of my sessions with Monica, I still found it very personal to talk candidly about my disability, but he was only a first grader; I wanted to honor his curiosity.

"I walk like that because I have something called 'cerebral palsy.' I know that's a big word. Can you all say 'cerebral palsy'?"

"Cerebral palsy!" my audience of first graders obediently chirped.

"Good job! You can call it 'CP' for short." The kids smiled back at me, glad they had said it right. "I want you all to make a fist with your left hand and then put your right hand around your wrist like this." I demonstrated this for the class until everyone was doing it correctly.

"When you move, your muscles get tight, like when you make a fist. Can you feel that in your wrist?" The students nodded. "When your muscles relax, it's like when you open your hand. Go ahead." I watched as 20-some first graders opened and clenched their fists, feeling their tendons move. "Some of the muscles in my legs don't ever relax; they are always tight like your clenched fist. That makes it harder for me to walk, and sometimes I trip and fall."

I saw a hand rise from the crowd. "Does it hurt?"

"No."

"Is it contagious?"

"Nope."

"Did you hurt yourself?"

"No, I was born with it."

As I scanned the reading well, looking for raised hands, I saw there were no more lingering questions, just smiling children, looking back at me, ready to learn. *Amazing. They like me even though I'm different.*

"Reminder of Library Materials Due." I rolled my eyes at the sight of this lingering message, once again sent to my inbox. It had been two weeks since I last clicked the renew button. *Ahhh...not yet!* I renewed Dave's book and then quickly deleted the e-mail before I had the chance to think about it again.

"Alex, I hear that you don't like to wear your leg brace."

"Uh-huh." Alex, an eight year-old I had met at church with CP stared up at me while we sat next to each other in the lobby one Sunday.

I nodded, knowing the feeling all too well. I hated wearing my braces growing up; they were sweaty and hot and didn't come in bright green like the one Alex wore. "I brought some pictures with me that you might want to see." I pulled out some black-and-white photographs that were taken for a newspaper article when I was four. "This is a picture of me when I was a little younger than you in physical therapy."

"Hey! I know that stretch!"

"Yes," I said smiling, "it's a hamstring stretch!" I pulled out another photo for Alex to see. "Here I am in my braces. They weren't as cool as yours, but I had to wear them for a while, just like you." Alex looked down at the photo and then looked up at me—unsure of what to say.

"Alex, if you ever want to talk to me about CP, or anything else, you can okay?"

"Okay," Alex looked down, shy to meet my gaze.

"Diary of a Wimpy Kid today huh Alex?" I said, seeing him carry in the book to the lobby the next Sunday on the way into church.

"Yes. I think it's funny."

"Me too!" I said, smiling. I scanned Alex's book then handed it back to him. "Do you have a favorite part?"

"Uhh...no, but....?"

"Yes?"

"Mmmm...what does it mean when this muscle hurts?" I looked down, Alex was pointing to his calf. I nodded to myself. A tightened calf muscle could be very uncomfortable.

I folded my arms and looked straight into Alex's eyes. "Alex, if you're in pain, I want you to tell your mom and dad, okay?"

"Okay."

"You have to promise me, if you're in pain, your parents need to know about it." Alex nodded, solemnly. "Alex, when my leg hurts like that, it usually means that I haven't stretched in a while," I said a little quieter so the conversation could be between just the two of us. "I can talk to you and your parents about how to stretch it later, okay?"

"Okay!" Alex whispered then turned to go into the sanctuary.

"Reminder of Library Materials Due." *Renew already!* I moved my mouse to click the blue link. A red message that I had never seen before scrolled across the top of my computer screen: "Cannot renew item. Renewal limit reached." *No! How is that possible? No one's even waiting for this book!* I looked at the record. It had been well over a month since I originally checked it out from the library; it had been hiding under my bed for weeks. "When is this due?" I looked at the box on the right—"Monday!?" It was already Friday afternoon. I couldn't put it off any longer—it was time to read *The Subtle Power of Spiritual Abuse*.

The weekend went by in a blur. After church on Sunday, I came home and fished the yellow book out from beneath my bed. I fanned the pages once, trying to get a feel for how long this would take. According to Amazon.com, I had 240 pages to read before I went to bed. "Alright," I told myself, "let's get this over with."

I sat on my couch for hours, pausing only to get a drink or use the bathroom. I spent a few hours sitting in my book nook, and as the sun went down, I ended up in my bedroom. As I neared the end of the book, my head hurt and my eyes were strained. Although I didn't understand it completely, reading the book gave me the language I needed to understand I had been abused.

I had experienced "scripture proofing," being told how to read the Bible in a certain way. So many people had told me that Jesus healed every person of their sicknesses, but I was sure that there were many crippled people on Earth the day Jesus went back to heaven. I had been told that I was entitled to my healing, except I couldn't exactly find that in the Bible either.

Dave's book had also talked about envisioning a distorted image of God. I felt quite certain that the way I pictured God had to be wrong. If I had to guess, I would have said that God looked something like Danny DeVito posing as a gym teacher in a blue polyester track suit with a whistle hanging around his neck. I was standing next to Him, exhausted by the calisthenics He had designed: push-ups, sit-ups, jumping jacks, and the list just continued to grow. God would love me and I could come close to Him when I got it right. But that was the problem; I could never get it right. I could never pray hard enough; I could never believe well enough. I wasn't good enough for God. That's why He hadn't healed me and that's why I had been so angry. I found an invitation at the end of the book to seek help. "It's okay to be needy..." I started at the book in my hand. *Really? It never seems okay in our culture to need anything, but if the pastor of my church is saying this, maybe I can go there and get help.*

Chapter 19

"Brad, we need to talk." After a failed attempt at reaching the 20-Somethings pastor on the phone, I approached him abruptly one evening as he was picking his daughter up from Open Door's mentoring program.

"Do you have time now?"

"Sure."

Brad peered around the corner, looking for a good place to talk. He opened the door to an empty classroom that was tucked away from the rest of the crowd. "Let's go in here."

I entered the room and sat down on a chair facing Brad. A cross I had seen used during communion on Sundays was sitting in the middle of the floor. Chairs were formed into circles where people had probably sat around in discussion. I looked ahead; traces of marker lined the whiteboard at the front of the room. The room seemed ordinary, and yet, sacred. *It's so private. Nobody's in here. Brad's not going to make me talk about this on a stage.* "This is a nice room."

"Yeah," Brad nodded, "we use it a lot." Brad and I made small talk for a few minutes before diving into the conversation. "What did you want to talk to me about, Jenny?"

I asked Brad if he had ever read Dave's book.

He nodded.

"I've experienced some of the things described in that book," I explained, "and I don't know what I should do now." I looked down at the floor, so solid under my feet—under all the turmoil inside me. "I've had some damaging church experiences that I've never talked about with anyone. I need to process what has happened to me."

"Can I ask what happened?" His tone was gentle, soft.

It was my turn to nod. I briefly shared my story. "Since then, my relationship with God has been raked over the coals; it has been shattered," I concluded.

In the silence that followed, I looked up, wary of how he was taking this all in. But Brad didn't look at me like I was crazy. He looked at me with compassion—he understood what I was talking about. "Jenny, God can use our deepest pain for His glory."

I tried to smile, "I know—and that's the only reason I'm talking to you right now.

"There are two resources that I can think of that may be helpful to you. One is a workshop that we offer once a year called *Restoring the Soul: Distorted Images of God.*"

That sounds interesting. I wonder what they'll say about Danny DeVito....

"It's a workshop where you can explore how you view God. It also gives you space to take those images to the cross, and let Him heal your mind." I stopped for a second and stared at the wooden cross standing in the middle of the room. Was that even possible? The idea of asking God to heal my thoughts when I was mad at Him for not healing my body sounded crazy, but I was desperate, so I would give it a try.

"The second resource is a ministry here called *Restoration through Prayer.* The people you meet with are not trained counselors, but they are available to help you process your church experiences and will pray with you as you seek God for healing." Memories of Monica's office flooded my mind, her hand over her mouth, gasping at what I revealed. Revisiting that memory was painful, but I hung onto hope. Maybe the people I would pray with wouldn't think I was crazy, maybe they would understand, like Brad.

I got busy working on my "homework." First on the list—*Restoration through Prayer.*

On a sunny autumn afternoon, I entered my church and found two women standing in the entryway, ready to pray for me. They didn't lead me to the stage; they took me to a private room, deeper and even more hidden than the classroom where Brad and I spoke. As we walked past empty cubicles to a small doorway, I wondered if God could find me when I was so tucked away. Would He hear my prayers for healing from a closet, with no microphones and an audience of only two?

I looked up at Rebecca and Tracy with uncertainty as I crossed the threshold. *Can we really do this in private? Are you sure that no one has to watch?*

"It's okay, have a seat."

I walked inside the room and sat down on a chair in the corner; a window was to my left and a table holding fountains and rocks was to my right. *Okay,* I told myself, *if this becomes unbearable, and I need to stare at something, I'll stare at that.* Monica's fish painting had carried me through counseling; perhaps the decorative rock that had the word "hope" engraved on it would help me through the next hour.

I started by telling Rebecca and Tracy about my background and my disability. I told them about Ian Parker and my desire for physical healing, feelings of shame and failure when it never happened, coping with these disappointments through academics in high school and college, dealing with my issues through intense counseling, attending the Beth Moore conference, and finally finding understanding from reading *The Subtle Power of Spiritual Abuse*.

After listening very intently and patiently to my story, Tracy turned her head, looked at me and asked, "Why are you here?" She paused for a moment, letting the question simmer. "What do you feel are the aftereffects of your spiritual abuse? It seems like you are doing well."

I was quiet for a moment as I felt my chest fill with pain. *Can't you see I'm wearing a mask!? Everybody thinks I'm doing well,"* I wanted to explain. *I don't even know what's wrong with me. My relationship with God...hurts.*

My lip started to quiver. I thought back to the night when my dad came home to take me to Ian Parker's meeting. My relationship with God at the time was tender, close, and innocent. Now we were like an old married couple, living in the same house, mad at the way life turned out—frustrated at the reality that there was no turning back the hands of time. It seemed as though that was how I was destined to live out the rest of my life with God, bitter and distant, but a deeper part of me longed to draw near.

"I just want my relationship with God to be the way it used to be," I said, swallowing the lump in my throat. It was so hard to hope when I knew all too well that sometimes hope gets crushed. "I used to know that I was His precious little girl, that He had a special place in His heart for me. I had a soft spot for Him too," my voice grew quiet. It felt awkward to speak of God with childish words, but that was the last time I could remember loving Him without pain.

Tracy nodded, seeming to understand what I was saying. "Let's start there," she said. "Why don't you begin praying?"

We have to pray now? I have to start? How could I possibly tell God how I felt? I bowed my head and sat silently for several moments, unsure of what else to do. With my eyes scrunched tight and my fingers folded neatly in my lap, I felt a flood of words bubbling up from my heart, but I couldn't let them spill from my lips. How could I tell the God I loved that I felt hurt by Him, that I felt betrayed? Could He ever understand how sorry I was for the way I acted, that I really did want to stop being bitter and angry so we could love each other again? Unable to voice such opposing emotions, my anger and love came out in tears. I started to weep quietly, but it wasn't enough. I let my mouth open up and began to sob.

Somewhere within the sound of my wailing, I heard Tracy's voice. "Can I put my hand on your shoulder?"

I nodded, still looking down. I could hardly see; pools of tears had clouded my eyes. My contact lenses were screaming in pain from all the irritation. Soon, I felt Tracy's hand embrace me. Then, she and Rebecca began to pray aloud. I couldn't find the words, so they offered theirs. In that moment, Tracy and Rebecca became midwives—helping me bear overwhelming pain to bring forth life.

"I'm so sorry God..." I began to pray aloud. "Please forgive me. I just want to love You again...."

"Where is your hope?" The question rang in my ears as I sat in the bucket seats in the back of the sanctuary later that evening, listening to Dave Johnson preach.

"If your relationship with God has been rocky, is rubble all you see, or do you see something more?"

I slid down in my seat and closed my eyes. I imagined rocky, broken ground, gray and desolate. Yes, that was what my relationship with God looked like, but maybe there was more to see. Could water come to heal the ground? Could plants start to creep up between the rocks?

I sat forward in my chair, opening my eyes to dig for my Bible. I opened it to Luke 15, pondering how I was like the Prodigal Son, on a journey home. I stopped when I got to verse 14: "After he had spent everything, there was a severe famine in the whole country and he began to be in need." I sat up and hugged my Bible into my chest, holding onto hope that seeing my broken ground would be the first step towards being held in a loving embrace. It seemed that somewhere off in the distance, if I really strained to hear, there was a voice calling to me: "Welcome home!"

Second on the list—attending the *Distorted Images of God Workshop*.

Two weeks after praying with Tracy and Rebecca, I found myself again sitting at a white table in another classroom at Open Door. It was a Saturday morning, and my coffee was in hand. Many of the people gathered in the room were at least twice my age, and everyone seemed to keep to themselves. It reminded me of how parents looked at UCP events, happy to have found help and understanding but still lamenting over the heartache that had brought them together.

Soon a pastor stepped up front, welcoming us and beginning the workshop. "If we're going to examine how we view God, we need to look at how we view our parents; oftentimes they mirror each other."

I sat back in my chair, thinking. When I was growing up, my parents had held the position that doctors had to earn their trust. After hearing the stories surrounding my premature birth, I couldn't blame them. When my mother was in labor with me, a doctor slipped into the room and offered an abortion. After a contentious exchange, she vehemently declined and I was soon delivered through an emergency C-Section. Later, when I was very much alive and recovering in the hospital's NICU, my mom was again approached by a social worker, suggesting that she attend a grief support group for mothers who are losing their children. She once again stood up for my life and boldly proclaimed, "My baby is going to *fight*, and she is going to live!"

It seemed that my parents' first reaction when someone was sick was to attempt to solve the issue on their own, considering all possible alternatives before going to the doctor. Partially because of this "can-do" attitude, I always pictured Jesus saying to me with a sneer, just like the Pharisees said to Him, "Physician, go heal Yourself." If I wanted healing, I was responsible for it.

"We created a folder for you today with some worksheets in it," the pastor continued. "We're going to give you some time right now to answer some of the questions." I looked at the teal folder in front of me. Inside was a salmon-colored sheet of copy paper with a question scrolled across the top: *How do you picture God today?*

I chuckled under my breath as I scribbled my answer. *I see God as Danny DeVito.* I put the back of the pen between my teeth and thought about the movie *Matilda* where DeVito plays a totally aloof dad: goofy, backwards, and corrupt. His genius daughter takes advantage of the situation and has a little fun replacing his shampoo with hair dye and gluing his hat to his head. The story is a hilarious reversal of parents who encourage the consumption of microwave dinners in front of the television and a kid who just can't get enough time to read. Frustrated by her intelligence, DeVito says to his daughter, "I'm smart and you're dumb; I'm right and you're wrong!"

As I sat at the table that day, I didn't so much think that God was asserting that I was dumb or wrong, just that I needed to work harder in order to somehow earn His love. I opened the journal that I had brought with me. About a month ago, I had made a list of all the things that I thought I should really try harder at in order to be a better person, a "good" Christian. There were many things on the list, some of them were typical: read my Bible every day, pray. Others were more routine: exercise daily, stretch, floss my teeth, take my vitamins, get eight hours of sleep. The list continued and, as I read it over, I decided that none of the things I had written in my notebook were bad by themselves; it was just that there were too many. They were overwhelming. I could do everything on the list for a day, maybe even a week, but trying to do it for my whole life was impossible, and if accomplishing everything was what it took to restore my relationship with God, it was never going to happen! I wrote on my paper in frustration: "What is this, some sick race without a finish line—no one is ever good enough?"

I looked around the room, hoping I could find someone to talk to. Tracy happened to be sitting in the back, open for conversation.

"Tracy, sometimes I think spiritual growth is an insult." She turned her head in curiosity, encouraging me to continue. I told her about my Danny DeVito analogy, that I had to work hard, do spiritual calisthenics in order to earn God's love. I confessed that I didn't delight in "being transformed into the image of God"; I felt burnt out by it. "Here, I made this list of things I feel like I need to do," I said, showing Tracy my journal, "I just can't do it all."

Tracy read a few items on my list to herself before looking up. "This idea that you have to work to earn God's love is part of the distortion you're experiencing."

"That's what I thought."

Tracy thought for a moment. Then she continued, "You're a teacher, right?"

"Yep."

"You don't look down on your students the first day of school because they don't know everything they're supposed to yet, do you?"

"No." My mind flashed to how dependent first graders were when they used the media center for the first time in the fall. Their tiny fingers could hardly reach across the keyboards to login. They struggled to check out books because they couldn't read the titles.

"You love them enough that you don't want them to stay where they're at for the whole year—you want them to learn and grow."

"That's true."

"God's like that, I think. He loves us where we are and delights as we change."

I nodded, thanking Tracy once again, but returned to my seat disappointed. The morning was quickly coming to a close and I felt like I had gotten nowhere. The final question written on my worksheet stared back at me, but I had nothing to write in response. *How might God be inviting you to view Him differently today?* I wanted so badly to see God differently, but I was stuck on the fact that I was running on a never-ending treadmill, exhausting myself, trying to reach God.

The ring of my cell phone startled me from my nap. The name sprawled across the screen surprised me. *Why is Denae calling me on a Saturday?*

"Hello?" I croaked out, my voice weak from sleep.

"Hello, Jennifer, this is Denae; sorry to call you like this," her voice came out in a rush. "I know you have a hair appointment scheduled for next week, but something came up and I have to go out of town. Can you come tonight instead?"

I rubbed my eyes, trying to comprehend her words, still groggy. "Yeah. I'll be there. I'll be coming right from the gym, so I might look a little sloppy."

"No problem. See you tonight!"

I rolled out of bed, pulling on my wind pants and an ugly gray sweatshirt that I had owned since high school. I laced up my pink tennis shoes and headed out the door. As I drove to the gym, I realized I hadn't showered that day; the morning had gotten away from me and now I was going to create even more sweat.

I climbed up on the treadmill, pounding the black belt with my feet over and over again. The shock from the motion climbed up my legs as I jarred my tightened calf muscles with each foot strike. I felt my lungs pound loudly in my chest, trying desperately to give enough oxygen to my overworked muscles. I pumped my arms, trying to relieve some of the stress in my legs, but I found myself gripping the side bars for support, losing my balance as my speed increased. I felt fatigued, flogged by the intensity of the exercise, but I kept going, ignoring every natural instinct in my body that was pleading me to stop. I would not relent, the desperate frustration I felt over wanting to see God propelled me forward. When I couldn't take it any longer, I stepped down and drove to Denae's house.

"Come on in, Jennifer!" I could hear Denae calling from the back of her salon. I walked through her hallway, pausing at the threshold as she turned around to look at me. If she was surprised by my disheveled state, at my audacity to enter a place where beauty was created wearing puffy eyes, greasy hair, and an offensive odor, Deane didn't show it.

"Have a seat!" Deane said with a smile as I climbed into her chair. She asked me about my day. Her tone was soothing, gentle, and soft. I told her a few things and while she was listening she took out a comb and straightened my hair, trying to determine how much needed to be cut.

"Let's get you cleansed." I laid my head back in her scrub sink and closed my eyes. *I love this part so much!* Denae's fingers massaged my scalp, moving in circles as the shampoo worked through my locks. A few minutes later, I heard Denae's voice calling me back from my state of bliss. "Ok, you can sit up now." I opened my eyes slowly, greeted by her smiling face.

Denae guided me back to the styling chair where she began to work very methodically, trimming split ends and creating new layers. Her eyes were focused and narrowed as she worked with her tools to snip, comb, and cut.

When it was all finished, Denae spun me around in the chair, facing the mirror. "What do you think?"

I looked in the mirror and couldn't help but smile. Denae's handiwork had transformed my image. For the first time that day, I no longer beheld a mess when I looked in the mirror. I was glowing and radiant, ready to face the world. "It looks great! Thank you—I needed that."

"My pleasure, come back any time."

I kept the radio off as I drove away down winding county roads, headed for home. About halfway there, I heard an inaudible whisper gently calling to me as I sat in my car. "If you want a picture of Me, think about what just happened."

"Oh!" I gasped, suddenly realizing the connection: Denae's call, waking me from my sleep, inviting me to come right away, even in my messy state, so I could be washed and transformed into something new. "Thank you, God!" I cried out in gratefulness. "I really wanted to see you today!" As soon I was home, I found my teal folder, pulled out my salmon- colored worksheet, and wrote the answer to the final question: *I learned today that God might not look like Danny DeVito in a blue polyester track suit, but He may actually look like my hair stylist Denae...*

Chapter 20

As I began to see God a little more clearly, I discovered that attending church became more of a delight. I gradually sat a little closer to the stage in the sanctuary, moving forward from my usual hiding place in the back. I didn't limit my time at church solely to Sunday morning. I came on Monday nights to 20-Somethings, Wednesdays for mentoring, and other times throughout the weekends for special events because church was slowly transforming from a place of pain to a place of healing in my life. After my encounter with Denae, I held onto hope that God was running towards me like the father of the prodigal son, eager to fulfill my desire to see Him more clearly.

Several weeks later, this hope seemed to be echoed in Steve Wiens' opening prayer one Sunday: "Jesus, give us the gift of seeing You in such a way that You captivate us."

"Please God," I prayed in my seat, hands folded on my lap, eyes squeezed tightly, "I want to see you." I also wanted to see Steve Wiens as a likable person as I watched him preach in his trademark black shirt, dark jeans, and trendy glasses. But as he gave his opening remarks all I could see was the scene from mentor training playing over and over again in my head. Oh how great it would have been to shed my disability like an oversized shirt, changing into what other people expected me to be overnight. My whole story would have changed because school would have been different. I would have had friends, I would have gone out for sports, I would have been able to ride the "normal" curve—a place Steve seemed to be riding with joy. I wish he understood, I thought as I unfolded my bulletin, ready to take notes. My mind shifted, thinking back to my youth pastor John Peterson, how I wanted a partner to walk with me on my journey...his silence...my heartbreak.

"Alright! Open your Bibles to Colossians, chapter 1!" Papers rustled throughout the room as people flipped through their pages. Dave Johnson and Steve Wiens had preached through a series called "The Way of the Rabbi" for two years, teaching about the Beatitudes, and had recently begun a journey through the book of Colossians.

Steve began to read the opening verses of the chapter, adding details about what was going on in Colossae during the time the book was written. Normal people went about their day living and working in a society that was overshadowed by the rule of Rome. Caesar had promised peace would reign through an agreement called the *Pax Romana*.

Pictures of "Little Caesar" danced in my head. I could see the animated character walking across the bottom of the TV screen in his toga and laurel leaf. He always stuck his javelin in the ground and called out "Pizza! Pizza!" like an automated bird while his pies spun around on the stick. I smiled at the thought.

Steve continued, "The thing that held everything together in Colossae was in Caesar. It's a powerful thing to be in something. We all have our little stories. These stories shape our character and set the direction of how we behave and how we think, and the biggest ones can even overtake us."

I scanned the stage. It looked different today. A whiteboard mounted on an easel was standing on the left. Steve walked over to it, picked up a black marker, and began to draw.

"So with the help of this whiteboard here and my *amazing* artistic capabilities," Steve paused, hoping people would catch his drift, "which Dave made fun of last night, by the way, which he should have because they're terrible... nonetheless, we're going after it!" Polite laughter erupted. I leaned closer in my seat, curious.

"I'm drawing a little picture of a man here. We're going to give him some glasses and some curly hair...receding." Steve continued to gather goodwill from the crowd. "Little soul patch—all gray." His marker continued to work until his self-portrait was complete. "Lots of little stories happened in my life. And one of them was that I was a severe stutterer when I was growing up—until about age 12 or 13."

"Ah!" I quietly gasped, coving my mouth with my hand. In that moment, I started to realize what Monica must have felt when I revealed the details of my past. *No way!*

"When I was little, I could barely get a word out. That affected my character, how I thought, how people treated me, how I thought people treated me—it was a big deal."

He preaches...every weekend...to thousands. Steve continued telling his story: moving to Belgium as a teenager, getting married, becoming a pastor. "Then we started to try to have kids, and a few years into it we found out we were struggling with infertility. And we did that for seven years."

I sat back in my seat, shocked at how wrongfully I had judged the man in front of me.

"Those seven years were incredibly marking in terms of our behavior and way we thought about each other and thought about God."

"Seven years," I whispered to myself quietly. I thought about my own wrestle with God that had also lasted just over a decade, littered with high hopes, heavy disappointments, and an uncertain future.

"We also started asking the 'Why God?' questions. When things got raw and politeness would leave our faces, we would say things like, 'Why are you doing this to us, God?' We would just get angry. It didn't seem fair."

As I sat in my seat, I realized that not only did Steve understand what it was to have a physical difference, but he also understood what it was to wrestle with God. Although tears never stained my cheeks as I sat in church that morning, in my heart I began to weep. *He understands! Oh God!*

"In our anguish and our pain, we experienced a God who was intimately with us and holding us together without any promise that infertility would go away."

I sat back in my chair and let the truth of Steve's words into my heart. I allowed myself to feel God's everlasting arms holding me together. I felt secure, not only in the presence of God, but also in the familiarity of the embrace. That morning, I quietly began to realize that God had been holding me together throughout my journey, without any promise that cerebral palsy would ever go away.

After the service, I wrote an e-mail to Steve, apologizing for judging him, thanking him for sharing his story, and telling him a bit of my own. I couldn't seem to type fast enough; a confession was pouring out of my heart into words.

One night after mentoring, Steve sought me out in the middle of teenagers and 20- somethings swarming Open Door's entryway and we talked face to face. "I don't know how it is to have CP, but the hardest thing for me about stuttering was that it was so public."

I stared up at him for a second, unsure how to respond. I found myself trying to swallow the surprise that Steve Wiens was no longer standing on a stage rows ahead of me, wearing a microphone, and preaching a sermon. He actually took the time to find me in the midst of a busy crowd, offering a piece of his own story before asking me to share more of mine. The fact that he could summarize the whole problem of physical disability in a sentence was even more shocking.

"Yeah," I said, nodding in agreement, "that's the whole problem. So often people want to know why I walk the way I do, but they don't want to get to know me for who I am."

"I read your e-mail, but I'd like to know more of your story." Steve looked at me, waiting for me to speak. I looked around—people were everywhere, some it seemed were waiting to talk to Steve.

"I'll write it out for you!" I said in a rush. *Where did that come from?* Steve seemed to have the same reaction.

"Ok," he said, my response taking him a little off guard. I wasn't going to give him the information he was seeking just yet.

"Yeah, that's what I'll do," I said, still trying to convince myself that this was a good idea. Steve had taken the time to find me personally, but I was at a loss for words. With all the people roaming around, it didn't seem like the time or the place to tell my story. I needed time and space to think. I told Steve I'd get it to him sometime that weekend, but as soon as I got in my car, I raced home as fast as I could and turned on my computer.

In great detail, I began to pour out my soul onto the page. I told of my premature birth, diagnosis, search for healing, and the resulting feelings of betrayal. I told him about trying to cope with academics, journeying through counseling, and finding help at Open Door. As I sent it off in the wee hours of the morning, I drifted to sleep grateful that I finally had a story to tell.

Weeks later, I felt my heart pounding as I opened up an e-mail from Steve Wiens titled *Big Question*.

"Jenny, I'm preaching this weekend on the process of character formation. My central premise is going to be that character is primarily formed in us through suffering. Would you be willing to let me interview you at the conclusion of my message, up on stage, for all three services this weekend? I think your story could be a powerful, real-life example of someone who is experiencing profound character formation as you have wrestled with God in the midst of cerebral palsy. Think about it and let me know!"

I read this e-mail and accepted the invitation to speak with a wide mix of emotions. At the height of believing that God was going to heal me, I held this dream in my heart that one day I would flawlessly walk across a stage, standing in front of many, showing the scars on my legs, sharing how I no longer walked with a limp, but because of my faith in God, I was miraculously healed of cerebral palsy. This dream died somewhere along the course of my journey with God. In the process, the stage transformed from a place of dreams to one of devastation. It was the backdrop to a story where a little girl's hope was increasingly elevated and then cruelly destroyed. It was where I denied my CP to achieve academic recognition and success. It was where I worked so hard to do everything right to somehow earn my healing. But despite all my perfect performances, the stage remained a place of shame, a place of confusion. So where was God and why didn't He heal me? Didn't He hear my desperate cry for His intervention? I was willing to do *anything* in front of *anyone* if only He would reach out and touch my body. I had kicked and screamed, cried and prayed. Stumbled and succeeded.

It was with these thoughts and memories in mind that I sat reflecting in the auditorium chairs near the stage of my church as I waited to share my story. It was hard for me to grasp that so much had happened in my life to get me to the point where I was sitting that morning. Was it possible that what I had dreamed as a little girl was somehow being fulfilled? True, I would never flawlessly walk across a stage in praise of a miraculous physical healing, but perhaps the scars on my legs bore a testimony of a different nature.

The scars, which line my legs, were the result of being under the care of a compassionate and skilled physician, Dr. Koop. His work didn't cure my condition or deliver me from cerebral palsy; it simply enabled me to walk more gracefully in spite of the tension caused by my tight muscles. I am forever marked by his work. Likewise, I have also been under the tender care of the Great Physician. His work has also not delivered me from my disability, but He has skillfully stitched the wounds of my heart back together. His repairs have allowed me to walk more gracefully with Him in spite of the tension caused by my unanswered questions. I am forever marked by His work.

Suddenly, my thoughts of comparison were interrupted by Steve's voice giving my introduction. "I want to invite a friend of mine up as we wrap up here. Her name is Jenny Hill. Jenny has been coming to Open Door for a few years. She is a mentor in the Next Gen program, a teacher, and she also has cerebral palsy. So, I asked her to share with us a little bit about life with cerebral palsy and what that is like. Jenny, Hi!"

I climbed the steps of the stage, walked over to a wooden stool, and sat next to my pastor. With great care, Steve asked me questions and, unlike our conversation in the entryway of our church, I was not at a loss for words. I opened my mouth and began to speak. From the depths of my soul, I ripped open my heart and poured out my story for all to hear. Steve started by asking me to tell what cerebral palsy was, so that the audience would know. I used the whole phrase, "cerebral palsy," holding nothing back as I spoke openly about my premature birth, disability, and struggles through school. I wasn't shy about what it was like to watch my peers play sports while I sat on the sidelines or the disappointing heartache I experienced when I was wasn't healed and people told me to "pray harder!" I finished by sharing how I was starting to see God at work in the midst of my disability, giving me unexpected empathy for others. I poured my heart out until my time was up; I had nothing left. After the service, I went home and hid under a blanket, trying to recover from all the vulnerabilities I had just unveiled.

That very public interaction was unlike those I had experienced before. Instead of humiliation, that interview was conducted with respect from someone I trusted. Instead of expressing confusion over the answers I had searched for throughout the years, I was able to express clearly that I had found a place of peace with God while living with deep questions. I still felt a profound sense of failure over the ending of my story and often found myself striving towards achievement and recognition in order to cope. However, that morning I was asked onto the stage not because of anything I had done or failed to do but because of the grace of God. He didn't see me as a failure or as an achiever, but simply His beloved Jenny. The interview didn't end with familiar feelings of shame over having to speak publicly of my condition and its limitations, but rather with the honor of a standing ovation.

When the message concluded, a few people came forward and invited me to speak at their venues. I was honored and floored at their requests. Not only had God been redeeming the stage, but He was also at work redeeming my voice. Those hard, painful days of counseling were serving a purpose. My voice on this subject would no longer be a desperate and defiant cry of anger and frustration towards a God who seemingly chose not to intervene or a voice silenced under the weight of shame. Instead, I could offer my voice and share my story as a means of an invitation; inviting people to pursue the struggle of becoming fully alive in God!

Made in the USA
Charleston, SC
13 April 2014